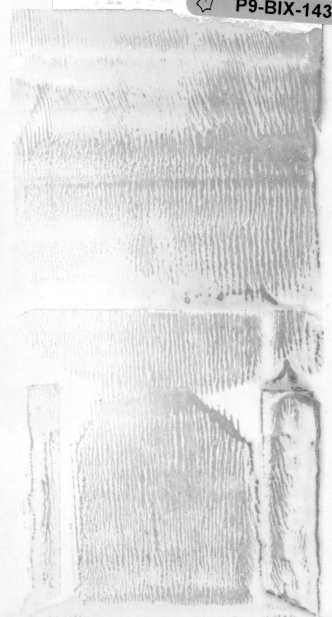

Our Debt to Greece and Rome

GEORGE DEPUE HADZSITS, PH.D.

DAVID MOORE ROBINSON, PH.D., LL.D.

ARISTOTELIANISM

BY

JOHN LEOFRIC STOCKS

PROFESSOR OF PHILOSOPHY

COOPER SQUARE PUBLISHERS, INC.

NEW YORK

1963

Published 1963 by Cooper Square Publishers, Inc.
59 Fourth Avenue, New York 3, N. Y.
Library of Congress Catalog Card No. 63-10300

AUTHOR'S PREFACE

SOME apology seems to be required for the form of this essay, which so far departs from the scheme of the series that the account of the author under discussion occupies the greater part of it and the account of his influence takes a secondary place. But the full story of Aristotle's influence would be a history of European thought, demanding an encyclopaedic knowledge which the present writer is far from possessing; and the only practicable alternative approach would appear to be through Aristotle's writings. This route therefore the writer has chosen. If in his choice of topics or in his presentation of the doctrine he should appear to any fellow student of Aristotle to have been arbitrary or capricious, he can only plead in self-defence the limitations of space and the necessity of simplification, and ask that his work may be judged only as an introductory sketch to a great subject.

CONTENTS

ARISTOTELIANISM

"What we seek is the cause; that is, the form."
ARISTOTLE, *Metaphysics*.

ARISTOTELIANISM

I. PROLOGUE

1. BIOGRAPHICAL

SOME two hundred years of free and fruitful speculation had already laid the foundations of science and philosophy when Aristotle succeeded to the leadership of Greek thought. The Greek colonies of the East and of the West had long ago completed their contribution. Their great men, Thales, Anaximander, Anaximenes, Heraclitus, Pythagoras, Parmenides, Empedocles, had now become figures of legend and pious memory. The new inspiration brought by Socrates, above all the great work of Plato and his Academy, had already won for Athens the speculative primacy which she retained for nearly a thousand years. An external observer, noting the variety of sects which professed allegiance to this inspiration, might have been excused for thinking that the new movement had been merely disruptive and revolutionary in tendency. Socrates himself, if Plato's evidence is to be trusted, claimed independence of his predecessors, and offered his own suggestions as a temporary makeshift to men in danger of complete shipwreck. But whatever Socrates thought, and whatever his other followers preached, Plato's foundation of the Academy in 387 B.C. was the prelude to an effort of concentration probably without parallel in the world's history. It is no undeserved accident that to posterity, beside the work of the early Academy and Lyceum, the efforts of other depositaries of the Socratic wisdom vanish utterly, like stars beside the sun. For it was the wisdom of Greece that was collected and distilled in those two great laboratories: in them, with insignificant exceptions, all streams met; and, in spite of all subsequent developments, in spite of the efforts of Stoics and Epicureans and Neo-Platonists, of atomists, physicians, and mathematicians, it was Aristotle after all who became in the end 'the philosopher' to the Christian world.

When Aristotle was born, Socrates had been dead 15 years, Plato was 43, and the Academy had already been in existence for a year or two. The bare facts of his life are these. His

father, Nicomachus, was court physician to
the father of Philip of Macedon; and Aristotle's early years were spent in the little town
of Stageirus in the Thracian Chalcidice. At
the age of 18, refusing to follow the ancestral
calling of physician, he migrated to Athens,
where he lived for 20 years as a member of
Plato's Academy. Then the master died, and
Aristotle left Athens. After four years on the
Asiatic coast, where he was for three years the
guest of a fellow Platonist named Hermeias,
ruler of Assos and Atarneus in Mysia (Aristotle had family connections in these parts),
he was called by Philip to Macedon to take
charge of the education of the young Alexander, then 13 years old. Aristotle stayed
with Philip until his death, seven years later,
and remained at the Macedonian court for
about a year after Alexander's accession to
the throne. It is sad that no reliable records
have survived of this experience. All we
know is that in 335–4 Aristotle returned to
Athens and founded a school of his own in
the Lyceum. This school he directed for 12
years, when the threat of prosecution for im-
piety, the real reason for which was probably
his friendship with the Macedonian Antipater,

made him seek voluntary exile in Euboea; and there within a year he died in the sixty-third year of his age.

The School which Aristotle founded was formed, after the model of Plato's Academy, as a religious brotherhood. The founder was its Head and had as his colleagues and assistants a number of men of proved capacity as teachers and investigators corresponding to the Fellows of an Oxford or Cambridge College. Aristotle, as a foreigner, was unable to own real property in Athens; but not long after his death the buildings and precincts became the property of the School, and probably the Fellows or 'Elders' had the right of electing their own Head. The religious bond was the cult of the Muses, solemnly celebrated on the last day of each month in a reunion of the whole School. The Fellows took it in turn to preside over the monthly Symposium, and the President of the month was also Dean, responsible for the discipline of the Students. Neither he nor the Head of the School seems to have received any fees from students, but a small subscription was demanded for the Symposium, the balance required for the entertainment being found by the President.

[6]

Certain religious duties also fell in turn to the Elders, and these too seem to have involved some expenditure. It seems therefore that private means were more indispensable to the Fellows than to the Students of the Lyceum.[1]

Personally Aristotle is said to have been something of a dandy and fond of good living. He was no doubt a man of the world, and may well have suggested in his appearance the adviser of kings rather than the distraught philosopher. If he was fastidious in his way of life and particular about appearances, that is as true to the counsels of his *Ethics* as the punctilious piety with which he seems always to have treated his friends and family.

Aristotle was a prolific writer, and his literary reputation stood high in antiquity: but by a curious chance the works, written for general circulation, on which this reputation was based have (apart from a few fragments preserved in other authors) entirely perished. They were, it seems, mainly dialogues, after the Platonic precedent, dealing with philosophical subjects in a fashion suitable to an educated public. What has survived is a mass of material plainly designed for the study and instruction of the School, including careful and abstruse lectures side by side with systematic collections of observations and long lists of questions demanding solution. The degree of literary finish varies very greatly in different works, and even in different parts of one and the same enquiry. These surviving works [2] classify themselves naturally according to subject as follows:

1. Logic. A number of treatises of unequal value, but containing in the theory of the demonstrative syllogism one of Aristotle's greatest contributions to the wisdom of the world.

2. The Theory of Matter and Motion. In four works, (*Physica, De Caelo, De Generatione et Corruptione, Meteorologica*) the structure of the physical universe and the various motions and changes of its parts are elucidated. Both the principles and the methods employed are apt to seem misleading or misplaced to a modern reader; but the first and third of these contain some of Aristotle's acutest speculation, and the account of the heavenly bodies in the *De Caelo* cannot be ignored in any estimate of Aristotle's view of the world.

3. The Theory of Life. The *De Anima,* with

the shorter treatises attached to it, expounds
the nature of soul as the principle of life dom-
inating organic matter.

4. The Animal World. The four treatises
on animals form the largest homogeneous mass
in the whole series. They are also the least
theoretical section of the corpus. Of all Aristotle's works these come nearest to the modern
scientific spirit. They have delighted natural-
ists of a later day. Darwin [3] wrote in a letter
of one of them: "Linnaeus and Cuvier have
been my two gods, though in very different
ways, but they were mere schoolboys to old
Aristotle."

5. Man and his Works. Under this head
come, first, the two works of Aristotle which
have had the widest influence in the modern
world, the *Ethics* and the *Politics*. Both works
are marred by a certain lack of unity and con-
secution; but though commentary is piled on
commentary and critics are always ready for
a fresh dissection, both works retain their
unexhausted freshness and suggestiveness,
alike for the student of Greek life, for the
ethical and political philosopher, and for the
mere man of affairs. With these two great
works may be reckoned, secondly, the *Rhetoric*,

which is now rather out of favour, though it was formerly well-known to students of the classics, and the *Poetics*, which expounds the theory of the Attic Drama, and has probably had more influence than any other single theoretical work on modern literary practice and criticism. In the field of Politics Aristotle is known to have collected or composed a series of treatises on the constitutions of the leading Greek cities. Of this series, one specimen survives, the treatise on the constitution of Athens.

6. Metaphysics. This title stands at the head of one of Aristotle's longest treatises, a name invented by Aristotle's successors to cover those discussions, called by himself 'Theology' or 'First Philosophy,' which had for subject the ultimate nature of being and the nature of the ultimate being. The work as it stands is not a consecutive treatise; but most of it is directly relevant to this purpose. Of Aristotle's 'metaphysics,' in the modern sense of the word, much is expounded in other treatises, particularly in the *Physics*.

The mere recital of such a list as this is sufficiently impressive. But, if one takes into account two facts, first, that all the works which Aristotle wrote for a wider public have been lost, and, secondly, that those which survive are expressed with a conciseness which often makes a sentence seem the equivalent of a paragraph and the paragraph of a chapter, one is even more amazed at the fertility of Aristotle's genius. The highly productive mind is apt to pay the price in a certain looseness of texture and lack of definition; but no such compensating weaknesses can be charged against Aristotle. No author has ever written with a more scrupulous exactitude or with stricter consistency. And all this work he had completed by the age of 62, by the time his Lyceum was only 12 years old.[4]

The School founded by Aristotle at Athens lived for over eight hundred and sixty years. When it was finally suppressed, in the sixth century of our era, by Justinian, it had a longer record of activity than any modern European University has at the present day. Aristotle of course on every side owed an immense debt to the Academy, a debt of which he was himself evidently conscious. He would have been proud, no doubt, to be called, as in later days he was, 'the most authentic of Plato's pupils.' But in Aristotle's works, and in the rather scanty records which survive of the early Lyceum, there are signs of a new and original spirit, sufficient in itself, quite apart from any divergence of doctrine, to differentiate the younger from the older school. The proneness to premature and fanciful speculation which marks the brave beginnings of systematic thought is beginning to be replaced by that impersonal sobriety and objectivity which is the condition of the coöperation of learned men. The gradual advance by coöperative effort which is the familiar characteristic of modern science, is plainly foreshadowed by Aristotle's work in more than one field; and though the Peripatetic school failed to retain this character for long after its founder's death, and no other philosophic school followed Aristotle's lead, it is here rather than in any doctrine that the distinctive mark of the Lyceum is to be found. Under Aristotle and his immediate successors the Lyceum was before all else the home of learning. " Aristotle," says Strabo,[5] " made all his pupils learned "; but he adds that Theophrastus, Aristotle's immediate successor as head of the school, was the most learned of them all.

2. THE SOCRATIC SUCCESSION

IT has already been suggested that the succession Socrates — Plato — Aristotle has a real unity, and that in Aristotle's work is to be found in a comprehensive sense the fulfilment of the Socratic impulse. In order therefore to appreciate the leading ideas of Aristotle's philosophy, we must consider this succession more nearly. But it is necessary to warn the reader that the difficulties are great, chiefly because of the gaps in our tradition. In spite of a general agreement that Plato was the truest Socratic and Aristotle the truest Platonist, there is no approach to unanimity among scholars as to the precise character of Plato's debt to Socrates, and little more as to Aristotle's debt to the Academy. Socrates wrote nothing: Plato wrote dialogues, which have survived, and gave systematic lectures in the Academy, of which the scanty indications furnished by Aristotle are practically the only reliable evidence. Aristotle's published works, belonging no doubt mainly to the earlier Academic period, have perished, and in his case we are dealing with lectures and other teaching material put together and worked up in and for the Peripatetic school. Thus the chief evidence for the opinions of Socrates is to be sought in Plato, and the chief evidence for Plato's later teaching is to be sought in Aristotle. It should also be noted that the period of time covered by this succession is a long one. Plato was 41 years younger than Socrates and was only 28 when the latter died: Aristotle was 43 years younger than Plato and cannot have seen him before Plato was 60 years old. A rough modern parallel is the succession of Jeremy Bentham (1748–1832), John Stuart Mill (1806–1873), Leslie Stephen (1840–1904). Suppose that Bentham had written nothing; that Mill's surviving works were dialogues, with an undefined margin of fiction, in which Bentham nearly always played the leading rôle, and when he was absent was never mentioned; that Leslie Stephen was an independent pupil of Mill's, and the systematic philosopher instead of merely the historian of the Utilitarian movement. Add an almost complete absense, unlikely under modern conditions, of independent evidence. What hope should we have of determining the precise relations of the three thinkers? Lifetimes covering a century and a half of change, direct evidence defective, indirect, scanty and unreliable — it is not surprising that the problem is difficult.

It would be foolish to attempt a solution of the problem in this place. An attempt to suggest Aristotle's historical context is, however, necessary. Here, then, is a statement, purporting to be historical, put by Plato [6] into the mouth of Socrates, an incident in the discussion which the hemlock brought to an end.

"In my youth," says Socrates, "I fell in love with natural philosophy. It must be splendid, I thought, to know the reasons of everything, why it comes to be and passes away, and why it exists. I used to puzzle myself with all manner of questions of this order, how some ferment in the warm and the cold makes these fit nutriment for animal life; whether it is blood or air or fire that makes thought possible, or perhaps rather the brain, by retaining and elaborating the sensations which it supplies. I used to wonder how all these things perish, and about the phenomena of the heaven and of the earth. But in the end I convinced myself that I was quite incompetent for such enquiries. They seemed to make me blind, so that I ceased to know even what I thought I knew before. . . . I have now convinced myself that by this method no account can be given of why things come to be and pass away and exist. So I reject it; and my clumsy efforts now follow a plan of my own.

"Once I heard a man reading from a book, which he said was by Anaxagoras. 'Thought rules,' he read, 'and is the reason of everything.' Here was a reason I welcomed. I felt I should be satisfied if thought explained everything. But I supposed I should be shown thought ordering each thing for the best, things coming to be and passing away and existing as it is best for them they should, no question considered but just this, what is best and most excellent. For the knowledge of this would, of course, include the knowledge of what is less good. So I had great hopes of Anaxagoras; and if he would explain, *e.g.*, the shape or position of the earth, by showing that it was better so, I was prepared to ask no other explanation. . . . I would not have sold my hopes for anything. I was all excitement to get his book and read it as quick as I could, so as to know with all speed what is best and what is less good.

"So it was a very high horse I fell from

when, as I read on, I found that my author
made no use of thought whatever in his explanations of the arrangement of the world,
but only of air and aether and water and other
such childishness. It was as if someone had
first said that all Socrates' actions are due to
thought, and then accounted for my present
behaviour by saying: 'Socrates is now sitting,
because his body is composed of bones and
sinews: these are distributed and related in
such and such fashions; and that is why his
legs are bent up under him as you now see
them.' As if he dealt on the same lines with
this discussion of ours, explaining by sound
and air and hearing, and throughout ignored
the true explanation, which is that the Athen-
ians have thought it better to condemn me,
and I have therefore thought it better to sit
here, juster to await the execution of the pen-
alty they have ordered. For, good heavens!
these bones and sinews would long ago have
been at Megara or in Boeotia, moved by the
thought of good, if I had not found it juster
and nobler to wait my execution than to run
away. It is surely no reason that this method
gives. It is true that without these things,
bones and sinews and the rest, I could not

carry out my resolves. But to find in them the reason of my doing what I do — I, whose conduct is due to thought — instead of in my choice of the best, is the idlest futility. It means incapacity to distinguish the reason of a thing from that without which the reason would be no reason. But indeed most people grope here in the dark, and take for reason what is no reason at all. They explain the position of the earth by a vortex or by its trough-like shape. They do not look for the force which keeps things as they are because it is best that they should be so. This is to them no force at all: their Atlas is stronger and more immortal. For myself, however, I would gladly be the disciple of one who could tell me of it. But here again I was foiled. I could not get on by myself, and I could not find anyone to teach me. So, as a second best, I devised for myself the method of explanation which I will now, if you like, describe.

"I thought after this that, being wearied by the study of things as they are, I had better take care not to hurt myself as observers of eclipses of the sun sometimes do. They are apt to ruin their sight, you know, unless they are content with a reflection in water or something similar. I was afraid that I might blind my soul by looking at things with my eyes and trying to grasp them by the senses. So I thought I must take refuge in theories (*logoi*), and consider the truth of things as reflected in them. My simile, however, does not altogether hold. I do not quite admit that to consider things in theories, as opposed to in fact, is to consider them in their reflections. Anyhow, this is the road I have taken. I start always from a theory, the strongest I can find, and what seems to accord with this I set down as true, whether in regard to reasons or any other matter, and what not as false. . . .

" It is really nothing novel. It is only what I have been saying the whole time, both in this and in previous discussions. If I am to tell you of the method of explanation I have worked out, I am brought back for my starting point to that well-known and hackneyed theme, the postulate of the existence of a Beautiful Itself, a Good, a Great, and so on. If you will grant me these, I hope from them to be able to explain the immortality of the soul."

In this very interesting passage a difficulty is created by the fact that the fundamental postulate referred to in the concluding sentences is the postulate of the existence of Forms or Ideas, advanced in practically identical terms in the *Phaedrus, Symposium* and *Republic*, and commonly, though not quite universally, supposed to be Plato's distinctive contribution to philosophy. But putting this crucial point aside, we note that Socrates represents his innovation as the attempt to introduce a novel kind of reason, and a new method of explanation. Three methods are sharply distinguished. The first, attributed to natural philosophy generally, appeals only to the characters and qualities of matter, warm, cold, dry, moist, etc., and seeks by means of these to explain such phenomena as nutrition and other kinds of change. The second, announced in a striking phrase by Anaxagoras, but neglected by him in fact for the first, is a simple and direct teleology, which has to show that all things are for the best, postulating necessarily a mind which rules the world and is satisfied with every detail in the field of its omnipotence. The third, Socrates' own poor effort, is elusively characterized. It is a second best, and yet it is not a second best; it is a falling back from the original to a reflection and yet after all its objects are not reflections. It finds in 'theories' the clue to the real, and the all-important 'theory,' the most unassailable that can be found, is the postulate of the existence of Forms such as Good, Beautiful, Great. These forms, Socrates goes on to say, provide the only kind of explanation which he can now accept. "All others I put on one side; they only puzzle me. In my artless and perhaps even foolish simplicity, I hug this to myself, that nothing else makes a thing beautiful but that Beautiful, by presence or participation or however else one may describe its advention. All I insist upon is this, that it is by the Beautiful that beautiful things are made beautiful." Here and nowhere else, he says, is safe ground.

It is interesting to compare with this statement the account which Aristotle gives at the beginning of his *Metaphysics* of the history of Greek thought prior to his time.[7] His account also turns generally on the principles of explanation employed. His view is that things are susceptible of precisely four kinds of explanation, all legitimate and necessary in their place; by their matter or physical constitution, by the impulse which set them upon a given track, by the purpose which they serve, and by the form which they embody. He was anxious to show that his predecessors had in some sense recognized all these four kinds of reason or cause; and he claims in his concluding paragraph to have shown this. All men seek them, he says, " but they seek them vaguely; and though in a sense they have all been spoken of before me, in a sense this is far from true. For the earliest philosophy in every sphere seems to lisp, as being young to begin with and only a first essay." In the course of his account, guided by this motive, he deals first with the earliest philosophers of whom he says (as Socrates of natural philosophy) that they had for the most part no conception of any but a material explanation of things; but he adds that, as enquiry proceeded, they were forced to look for an impulse to account for movement, and so tended to include the second of his types of explanation. In this category he includes the ' Thought' of Anaxagoras. The first approach to a notion of Form or Essence Aristotle finds in the Pythagoreans, and Plato's effort is represented as in principle a continuation of theirs. It is plainly implied that the all-important step forward made by Aristotle himself was the distinct formulation of this principle of explanation. For reasons not here relevant the Platonic Forms were inadequate.

The part attributed to Socrates and Plato in this development is outlined in the following paragraph. " After the systems we have named came the philosophy of Plato, in most respects following these thinkers (*viz.* the Pythagoreans) but possessing peculiarities that distinguished it from the philosophy of the Italians. For first, as a young man, Plato attached himself to Cratylus and the Heraclitean doctrine, that sensible things are ever in a state of flux and there is no knowledge about them; and these views he held unchanged to the end. Socrates, however, was occupied with ethics and not at all with nature in general, seeking here the universal; and Socrates so first drew attention to definitions. Plato, accepting his teaching, formed the view that these enquiries concerned not any sensible thing but entities of another kind, for the reason that the common definition could not be that of a sensible thing which was always changing. These entities he called Forms. Sensible things, he said, were beyond these, and named in every case after these;

for the many things bearing the Form's name existed by participation in it. In this, only the name ' participation ' was new. For the Pythagoreans say that things exist by ' imitation ' of numbers, and Plato, changing the name, says by participation. But what the participation or the imitation of the Forms might be they left an open question." A little further on it is noted that Plato utilized two of the four principles, form or essence, and matter; and elsewhere it is complained of him that he supplied no impulse to account for motion.

Much controversy has centered on this paragraph; and certainly there is room for difference of interpretation. But taken in the context already sketched, it seems at least to make Aristotle's theory of the development of which he regarded himself as the climax pretty clear. The Pythagoreans of Italy first vaguely adumbrated the notion of a ruling form, which the successive efforts of Socrates and Plato finally enabled Aristotle to bring to perfection. Socrates' service in this matter was the invention of scientific definition, but this powerful new weapon he himself employed only in the field of conduct. Plato was ready for a wider sweep: but first he asked what it was that was so firmly fixed and defined, so clearly grasped and known. Not, surely, the thing that is seen, the event that happens (for these refuse to remain to be so fixed and are always changing), and yet, something that has reference to these and explains their changes — a form or character, which things in experience are found temporarily and inadequately to suggest or represent. But knowledge is not knowledge unless what is known is real. Therefore it was the form known and defined that was real; and the visible thing that aped it was relatively unreal, real if at all, only in the degree of its success in receiving, or sharing in, the perfect and unchanging form. So Plato came to assert the existence of Forms superior to, and existing separately from, the things of common experience; but Aristotle complains that he never explained how the temporal order is able to ape, or mirror, or receive, or share in the eternal.

This short sketch of Aristotle's must certainly not be taken as an exhaustive account of the work of Socrates and Plato. It is written, as I have already tried to indicate, from a very definite standpoint with reference to a particuar ultimate problem. Its connection with the passage quoted from the *Phaedo* is so close that Aristotle can hardly have failed to have that passage in mind; but the two accounts are not easily reconciled if the Socrates of the *Phaedo* is substantially true to life. The Socrates of the dialogue is not occupied with definition in the field of conduct, and shows no hesitation in adopting as his main principle a postulate involving the very step which Aristotle attributes to Plato. The traditional view, seriously questioned only in quite recent times, supposes that the doctrines upheld by Plato's Socrates are substantially those of Plato himself, and that it is the philosophical development of Plato, not Socrates, that is described in the passage cited. This view is even now perhaps generally dominant; but it has not been wholly able to maintain itself in the face of modern criticism. The old orthodoxy supposed the theory of Forms to be wholly Platonic: the new heresy claims it as definitely Socratic.[8] The only result so far reached seems to be the negative one that all other evidence as to the teaching of Socrates except that of Plato (including Aristotle's) is practically worthless, so that the only hope of an answer to the question lies in a renewed scrutiny of the Platonic Dialogues. This is therefore the field in which the controversy is now mainly proceeding.

It is in no way necessary here to enter further into this dispute. For our present purpose it is of little importance where the line of division between Socrates and Plato is drawn. In general the story of the *Phaedo,* as far as it goes, corroborates by its emphasis on the supersession of the material cause, as well as by its indifference to the problem of a moving principle, the account given by Aristotle. Both invite us to take as a clue to the historical development of Greek thought the class of reasons adduced, the methods of explanation in use; and following either we should be necessarily led to regard as central in Aristotle's system the oft-repeated doctrine of the four reasons or causes (material, efficient, formal, final, as they are usually called); and of these four we should be plainly led, on the evidence of the *Phaedo* alone, to consider Form the most important; for Socrates' narrative places the good or final cause politely but plainly in the second place. And it is in fact true that Form is the central notion of Aristotle's philosophy. The last task of this introduction is

[27]

therefore to give a preliminary sketch of this central notion.

The commonest word for 'Form' in Aristotle's Greek, as well as in Plato's, is *eidos*. But Plato used also another word, *idea*, of closely related origin and meaning, which came through Latin into modern languages and has given to the Platonic theory its most familiar name. There would have been little harm in this name if modern philosophers had not succeeded in popularizing a totally different meaning of the word 'idea.' But, since this has happened, it is best, in order to avoid the subtle perversion of false associations, to give up the word in this connection and use the nearest English equivalent. Plato's great metaphysical postulate, then, was the existence of Forms, and the same term, we have already said, is central in Aristotle's philosophy. The evolution of this term, therefore, offers the most convenient path from the Academy to the Lyceum.

The typical Form in the surviving statements of the Platonic doctrine is a neuter adjective, and the adjective selected is a common predicate such as good, beautiful, just, equal, great. In the *Parmenides*,[9] where Plato makes the youthful Socrates state the doctrine to the aged Parmenides as a new-found novelty of his own, such instances are given first, and then, in reply to a question, Socrates professes uncertainty about such terms as man, fire, water: " I have often been puzzled," he says, " whether I ought to put them on the same footing as the others or not." In fact, in the Dialogues, instances of this kind — what the Logic of the Schools calls ' concrete general terms ' — are not adduced, with the exception that in two passages [10] a form is supposed, corresponding to an object made by man: ' bed ' is the instance in one case, ' shuttle ' in the other. It was the vision of the Form which made possible the artist's creation of the object. But no list of instances includes such objects side by side with simple attributes like good and equal; and neither of the two passages is primarily a statement of Plato's metaphysical or epistemological position. Further Aristotle says definitely that forms were not supposed corresponding to human constructions. On the other hand, Socrates' refusal to say either yes or no in the case of ' man ' and ' fire ' is consistent with the Dialogues to this extent, that the doctrine is defined by phrases

[29]

which in every case leave open the inclusion of such terms. The list of instances usually ends with an indefinite generalizing term ('and the like'); and Plato's language would naturally lead the reader to suppose that whenever the same name is applied in the same sense to a number of things there is at least a *prima facie* case for supposing a corresponding Form.

Parmenides in the Dialogue treats Socrates' hesitations as proofs of his immaturity. When he is older, he suggests, and more of a philosopher, he will be more consistent and thoroughgoing. It is natural to suppose that Plato followed the advice of the teacher for whom he professes such veneration. Anyhow in Aristotle's criticisms of the Platonic theory instances like 'animal' and 'man' are found side by side with 'good' and 'beautiful.' Restrictions are implied, *e.g.*, in regard to manufactured things, but they are of a comparatively minor order. Thus it appears that the philosophic notion of Form had a history which may be conjecturally reconstructed as follows. At first a form was primarily an atomic qualitative constituent of reality, analogous to the 'simple nature' of early modern philosophy; but it was not definitely restricted to this use, and for one reason or another Plato soon found himself forced to extend the notion to cover every authentic universal. It is possible, though not perhaps very likely, that at a certain period in Plato's development the simple attribute was replaced as typical instance by substantial complexes like man, horse, and other natural species. We know further from Aristotle [11] that there was a stage in the development of the doctrine in which the Forms were practically identified with or confined to numbers, and he distinguishes this from an 'original' version (*i.e.*, presumably, the version established in the Academy when he joined it), which postulated a Form for every universal.

All this may well seem too involved and in-conclusive to give much of a line for the interpretation of the Aristotelian doctrine; but it does at least yield an important negative result. The Platonic School, it seems, before Aristotle, did not regard Form as the constitutive principle of what we ordinarily call a thing, even though Forms were constitutive of reality. The final identification with numbers would surely have been quite impossible, if Form had been so conceived. The point of view must have been one from which the things of ordinary life are reduced to appearances, are seen as the product of a division, convenient no doubt for practical purposes, but not ultimately tenable. It is the consistent suggestion of such an attitude in the works of Plato which more than anything else creates the affinity between Platonism and modern Absolute Idealism; and the refusal to adopt it has enabled Aristotle, in spite of many daring flights of metaphysical fancy, to take his place among the great empiricists.

The Forms of Aristotle were no 'bloodless categories' whose unearthly ˉdance, grasped by pure thought, gave the lie to the deceits of sense: they were the real indwelling principles in the life and movement of things. Hence the detailed explanation of the facts of experience, which is for the Platonist an uninteresting or impossible task, becomes to the Aristotelian an absorbing pre-occupation.

Thus in Aristotle the Socratic movement completes its circle. The enquiries which Plato followed Socrates in rejecting, come to their own at last, but not by a simple swing of the pendulum or by surrender of other ground which the efforts of these thinkers had meantime conquered. Their conquests remained; and the great organizer of victory who completed their work thanked them for his opportunity. Aristotle merely played Alexander to Plato's Philip. As the pupil set out to conquer the inhabited world, the master settled in Athens to establish his dominion over the whole field of knowledge. It was one of those rare moments in history when barriers seem to fall, till the only limit is that set by shortness of life or weakness of will. Both pupil and master attempted, no doubt, more than they or anyone else could have been expected to perform; but each had more than enough success to justify him; and between them they secured for Hellenism the proudest triumph which the spirit of any race has ever enjoyed.

II. ARISTOTLE'S WORLD

1. FORM AND MATTER [12]

ARISTOTLE must now be taken to be speaking for himself.

When a thing is known it is known as a Form; and anything further known about it is known as dependent on this form. The form thus supplies the sole ground for the explanation and understanding of whatever can be understood or explained about a thing. But what is most known is most real. Therefore the primary reality is Forms, and any reality of lower degree is necessarily dependent on them. Form supplies the only satisfactory reason to the knowing mind, because it is the only active principle in the real world. Philosophy, therefore, which has the task of determining the fundamental nature of Being, without restriction to any special field or character, must before all else make clear the conception of Form.

The Form may be said in a sense truly to be the unit of being and of knowledge. But,

on the one hand, the forms do not just lie
side by side in a mere aggregate or heap, and
on the other their indivisibility does not pre-
clude a certain internal complexity. If they
were a mere aggregate of independent entities,
thought would proceed, presumably, by adding
one to one till the tale was exhausted; and if
they were quite simple and accepted no kind
of analysis, the most thought could do would
be to name them. But would things so simple
be capable of being even recognized and
named? What experience in fact presents us
with is an inexhaustible number of particular
things, which have been named and grouped
and classified in a variety of ways by past
generations. These divisions we accept in
learning and using language, and take for our
starting point when we indulge in systematic
or scientific thinking. It is among the inexhaustible particulars that we find our friends
and familiars, persons and animals and places
and possessions; but it is not these, not these
at least in their familiar aspect, that the common language knows. Language requires us
to force each of these familiars into line with
other unfamiliars as man, horse, dog, town,
and offers further manifold groupings more

general still, ending in great kingdoms like animal, vegetable, mineral. As applicable each to a number of particulars these terms are called universals. While man is *operating*, as statesman or producer or simply in the satisfaction of his own desires, he is dealing necessarily with particulars: and though in such activities, as we shall see, he would be powerless if he faced his situation merely as particular, yet a certain emphasis on particularity is inevitable. But man is no mere operator. He also desires to *know*, often no doubt only in order better to operate, but always to some extent also under no practical spur and with no idea of any profit to be got out of it, but just because knowledge attracts him, because he is so made. And man's thought, when directed upon knowledge, without reference to any operation, is found to concentrate wholly upon these universals. If the particulars are not ignored, their particularity is at least out of mind. The emphasis is reversed.

The desire for knowledge finds satisfaction in the systematic thought of science and philosophy. Each science takes a special field marked out by an all-pervading general character or kind, such as 'animal' or 'plant,' which it finds manifested in a great but exhaustible variety of alternatives, of which finally the inexhaustible variety of particulars are considered as instances. The general kind (genus) gives one limit; and the other limit is set by the fact that there is no knowledge of the particulars. The genus is said to be divided when alternatives are established within it. The products of division may be themselves divided, and at each step the number of particulars falling under each member is diminished: but this process has a natural and necessary end when the divisions arrived at are found to be not further divisible. Thought has then reached the indivisible species, repeated identically in particular things of which it is the form and essence. This form is known, but not proved, as a constituent of the genus: it is analyzed in definition as a particular modification of the general character: and forms so defined are the basis of all further procedure, their existence being assumed at the outset of the enquiry.

The Forms then are not independent of one another. Nor do they lack internal complexity. This is evident from the composite character of the definition, which states the genus, the system of which the given form is a constituent, and the difference, or peculiar constitutive character, in virtue of which the form is able to make its peculiar and unique contribution to that system. And there is also the complexity, which, though it is not part of the form and therefore not stated in the definition, follows from the form and belongs properly and necessarily to all things which exhibit it and to nothing else. This complexity it is the task of science to explore by means of the method called demonstration. In so doing it relies on certain principles common to all thought, such as the laws of contradiction and of excluded middle, on other principles common to a group of sciences (*e.g.*, to such as deal with quantity are common the axioms concerning quantities), as well as on principles, such as the definitions, peculiar to the field of investigation. The form of demonstration, the demonstrative syllogism, is the same in every science, and is further evidence of the unity of knowledge and of being. The sciences are not, any more than the forms, independent wholes lying side by side. The consequential attributes established by scientific deduction are called properties. Science may therefore be said to demonstrate the properties of the species of a genus in virtue of its knowledge of the forms and of their systematic interrelation, by means of a method common to all sciences and principles some of which are special, some common.

It should be added that, though things are known as forms, this knowledge does not by any means account for all the well-assured statements that can be made about things. The things which exhibit a given form have definite and describable differences from one another, which clearly cannot have their sole and complete ground in the form, because the form is in each the same and by itself accounts for no differences. A man is necessarily man, with the properties which that implies; and so far his nature is exhausted in propositions true of all men whatever: but he is also perhaps a poet or a statesman, bald or hairy, sitting or standing, of a certain age and origin. These attributes depend in varying degrees on conditions external to the form or essence. They are termed accidents ('incidents' would be perhaps nearer to the Greek). Considered from the standpoint of form, *i.e.*, scientifically, they are what *may* be, in opposition to the properties which *must* be, not necessary but contingent. As such, however well ascertained they may be in a particular case, their recognition cannot claim the name of knowledge, which is confined to the necessary and its grounds.

So much then for science. The foregoing outline of the notion applies in principle to all systematic thinking inspired simply by the desire to know. Science therefore is not distinguished from philosophy. But science includes three bodies of doctrine which exhibit important differences from one another, resulting from the differences of their subject-matters. These are physics, mathematics, and theology or 'first philosophy.' Mathematics is peculiar in that, by a kind of fiction, it treats as form and substance something which is not truly substantial but an attribute or adjective of substance, namely quantity. Theology is peculiar in that its subject is not a kingdom of the real, but the real itself in its innermost nature. It is not necessary to consider these peculiarities further at this point. Enough has been said to show that the three doctrines are not coördinate, and that the account above given could not be applied without certain qualifications to mathematics or theology.

The world then is a system of forms, presenting to the mind the intelligible diversity and ordered interrelation of members which the word system implies. But if it were only this, it would not also present itself as an inexhaustible multitude of particular things; there would be no time or space, no change, no imperfection. These familiar characters of experience cannot be simply set aside as unreal: they must be accounted for, even if the account is, as Plato's Pythagorean said,[13] in some sense spurious. And it must be spurious, it would seem: for they can clearly not be explained without surrender of the position that form supplies the only ground and reason.

The world of Nature is not only Form: it is also Matter. It consists of forms which can only exist as materialized or embodied. Hence the science of Nature has to do not with mere Form, but with formed matter, or bodies. In this principle, the complement in Nature of Form, is to be found in the last resort the ground of every character of the experienced world which Form is unable to supply. The existence of matter receptive of form accounts for the multitude of particulars, for their extension in space and time, for movement and change generally, and so for the indeterminate and approximate character of the things of this world at any moment of their existence. But before considering the world of Nature more closely, the reader is entitled to the warning that Nature is only one kind of being, and that its changing complex of matter and form would be impossible and inconceivable if there were not a world in which Form exists by itself in its own right.

The particular things, then, which fill the perceived world are specimens of formed matter. But it is a commonplace that they are in constant change, ' all flowing ' as Heraclitus said, and his judgement was endorsed by his successors. Their change is simply their effort to achieve perfection in their kind, to become in fact what in principle they always are, to reach their form. All change which is not degeneration or failure is the process by which the relatively unformed becomes formed. Thus change leads us to regard form in a new light, as an end to be attained, the content of a purpose implicit in the being of particular things. Something analogous to that which is recognized in human life as desire and purpose is operative throughout the world of nature. Each thing is striving to grow into the form which its matter is fitted to receive. The analysis of change thus gives us, first, Form, now seen as the goal of effort or end or good, the destined determination of a thing; secondly, Matter, which in general can only be described as the destined recipient of Form, or the indeterminate determinable; and lastly the thing itself whose continuing existence is all change and movement, movement however which is not random or purposeless (for Nature does nothing at hazard or in vain), but operated by Form itself as object of effort and desire. Though it is the nature of Matter to accept Form, as of Form to mould Matter, yet the domination of Form is never complete. Matter is the indeterminate, and the thing, which is material, can never achieve the complete definiteness which is the ideal goal of its efforts. However excellent it may be, what is will hint a might be, the actual will imply a potential, which if actualized would bring the goal nearer. The fact of change thus implies imperfection and indeterminateness in all natural things, and forces upon us the conception of potential being.

Now that which is potentially x is already actually y. It is not completely indeterminate, mere matter, but a thing, a complex of form and matter, qualified in a certain describable fashion. The earth which is made into a pot and the seed which later becomes a tree are definite entities, distinguishable from other things not merely by position in space but also by assignable characters, which are universal, as capable of indefinite repetition in other like instances, and are seen to make them suitable for the purpose for which man and nature are going to use them. But since the thing which is actually y (seed or clay) lacks the determination implied in x (tree or pot), and is destined to receive this determination, x may be described as the proper and proximate matter of y. In virtue of form already possessed it is seen to be proper to y, and the same reason justifies the qualification proximate. For the development of a thing is not the mere conversion by stages of the formless into the formed, but the superimposition of form upon form. Forms are higher and lower according to the character and complexity of the synthesis which they imply; but in all existent things we find in the last resort the same set of simple constituents, fire, air, water, and earth. These are already of course formed matter; otherwise they would not be different from one another. They are, as it were, the clay with which nature works. Behind these simple bodies, of which little speculative analysis is possible, lies the primary or ultimate matter, of which nothing whatever can be said, except that it receives form. Since it lacks all definite character, it is unknowable. It is a mere limit or residuum marking the place where analysis ends.

We thus obtain the vision of nature as a world, close-packed with a hierarchy of forms each capable of infinite repetition in particular things, and in every repetition renewing its never completely successful struggle to dominate matter. Absolutely, success is not achieved; but relative success (*i.e.*, a close approximation to form) must be regarded as the normal and natural case: otherwise the world would be chaotic. Approximation is closest where success is easiest, namely, in the lower orders of being. A piece of earth will practically always behave as earth should. In the higher realms of nature, of which these lower orders are the necessary basis and pre-condition, failure is much commoner. It is with Nature as with Man: the higher the task, the more difficult it is; the more complicated and laborious become the processes of fulfilment; the more frequent the disappointments. Nevertheless it is the passage to form and the features incidental to it which must be called natural: for the form is the essence and nature of the thing all the time. All else is failure and perversion, and must be called unnatural. We shall find that such deviation of nature, due to the successful resistence of matter to form, occurs sometimes on a large scale in the higher orders of being.[14] There are also many isolated occurrences, both good and bad, in the world of nature which must be ascribed to chance, since they follow paths of their own divergent from those of nature.

Nature, therefore, considered as a whole, is found on investigation to reveal a system which it does not fully express; a system which, because it is inevitably and endlessly yoked with inert Matter, is forced to take on the likeness of multitude and movement, to parcel itself out in space and time, to appear as a series of regular processes in which things come to be instead of being known as a system of timeless fact in which forms are. And even its regularities, as we have seen, are only approximate. The inertia of Matter sets a drag upon these processes, which operates unequally and incomprehensibly to frustrate and disturb the eternal design. But at the physical extremity of this world of bodies, a precious envelope enclosing it on every side, the hollow sphere of the heavens repeats, eternal and unchanging, its complicated motions, to show that in nature's crowning work some at least of these defects are removed. Here matter has lost its grossness. The simple bodies, earth, water, air and fire, of which all things below the heavens are composed, do not penetrate into this region. They are there replaced by a matter wholly receptive of form, of a fineness proportionate to its distance from our earth. As a result, the infinite repetition of form in passing particulars is here removed, with all its implications of process and composition: nothing unnatural ever occurs, but all is perfectly in accord with nature: regularity is absolute and unbroken. All that is left to indicate imperfection is the spatial movement itself. The material, however perfect it may be, can only exhibit form by means of movement; and movement, however regular, is a sign of imperfection.

Now it is an evident fact written large upon the face of experience if we look closely enough, that the existence of the perfect is a necessary condition of the existence of the imperfect. It is true of course that in any natural process of growth or development the imperfect precedes the perfect in time. There is first the egg and then the chicken; first the baby and only after many years the grown man. But it takes a grown hen to lay an egg and a grown man to beget a child. Thus even in time experience shows form achieved to precede the process by which form is achieved. If we attend to the implications of this fact, and reflect, further, that matter, space and time, and every form of movement are themselves evidence of imperfection; if we observe how in the world of nature the superior being of the heavens conditions and sustains by its eternal and unchanging movement the broken and disorderly movements of the earth, we find ourselves forced to pass in thought beyond nature and the evidence of our senses, and postulate pure Form, unmoved, spaceless and timeless, as the eternal support and condition of the restless movements of the material world. This Being immemorial tradition bids us recognize as God, and our own doctrine enables us to describe as form without matter, being without becoming, actuality without potentiality; and again, as spirit without body, intelligence without sense, activity without action or desire. And if it is asked how the unmoved can cause motion, the answer has already been given when we explained how forms, which are unmoved, are the active principle in the movement of things. This form also appears, in relation to the world of experience generally, as goal or end. God is the ultimate object of all this effort and desire. The movement of things is in the end nothing but the imitation of God.

" On this principle, then, depend the heavens and nature. His life is like ours at its short best. Such is his life always (which ours cannot be); for his activity is also pleasure. And while thought varies in perfection with its object, it is at its best and most divine when it is in such direct contact with its object that it and its object may be said to be identical.

This best and most perfect contemplation it is that God enjoys. If, then, with God it is always well, as with us sometimes, this is wonderful; and if even better, it is more wonderful still. And this is the fact. Life too is his: for the actuality of mind is life, and he is that actuality, an actuality which essentially is perfect and eternal life. We say, then, that God is a living being, eternal and perfect, and that continuous and eternal life and being are his. For he *is* this." [15]

2. The Simple Bodies [16]

A BODY is either simple or composite; and composite bodies are composed of simple bodies. The simple bodies in the world of change which occupies the centre of the physical universe are, as we have said, earth, water, air and fire — the four which Empedocles had designated as the elementary constituents of all things. The characteristics of these four elements, and of the fifth element of which the heavens are made, must now be considered in greater detail.

Earth, water, air and fire, though not of course divisible into bodies different from themselves, are yet analyzable by thought. They can be resolved into different groupings of the two pairs of contraries, warm and cold, dry and moist. Earth is cold and dry, water cold and moist, air warm and moist, fire warm and dry. In this series each term has one quality in common with its neighbour, and in respect of its other fundamental it is contrarily qualified. This explains the constant interchange which is observed to take place between them: the solid melts, the liquid evaporates in air, and the vapours feed the flames. Change is the replacement in a body of contrary by contrary quality: and while each element can therefore pass into any other, transformation is easiest and quickest where the two terms have one quality in common. The four elements thus present us with an unending cyclical process of change, characterized by the alternation of contrary qualities in their two pairs, warm and cold, dry and moist. The bodies are the bodies we perceive in experience, and their qualities are the qualities apprehended through our sense of touch: but experience never in fact gives them in their purity. This is particularly obvious in the case of fire. The flame we see is no stably organized material, but a phenomenon of transformation in which the warm and dry substance which is fire is being generated.

These bodies are not inert, requiring to be moved mechanically by an impulse from without. The ultimate matter, from which reflection derives them, must no doubt be conceived as inert; but each of them has a movement of its own, by which, like any other natural thing, it seeks to complete its form. It is evident to observation that, where there is no obstacle, earth moves in a straight line downwards and fire in a straight line upwards. And since the physical universe is a sphere, 'downwards' will mean towards the centre of this sphere, and 'upwards' towards the circumference. Water and air move with the same motion as earth and fire respectively but with less persistence. Now this inherent impulse to move is unintelligible unless it has not merely an actual but a natural limit. We must not suppose, therefore, that earth and fire simply continue to move until they are stopped. We must rather suppose that there is for each a place on reaching which the impulse would be satisfied, so that they would cease to move, and rest in the completion of their nature.

We must say then that each element has its natural place or home, and that its movement is the effort to reach this. But this is only fully true of earth and fire, each of which has an exactly determined goal to its movement. The two intermediate bodies, water and air, are less determinate both in themselves and in their movement. Their movements reach their goal in a place which can only be defined by the boundaries of the bodies next them. These facts may be otherwise stated by means of the terms heavy and light. Democritus and other earlier writers maintained that this distinction was only relative. They were wrong. The distinction in the case of the two extreme bodies is absolute, since the one moves downwards and the other upwards to a defined goal. It is only in their application to the intermediate bodies that the terms become relative. Each of these is both heavy and light.

It must be noted that this scheme cannot be made perfectly symmetrical. In its own place a body should be neither heavy nor light: it should be perfectly at rest. This is in fact the case with earth and fire, but not with the intermediate bodies. Water, though it has been said to be light as well as heavy, and to have its natural place above earth, would nevertheless continue to move downward if the earth below it were withdrawn. And air is only relatively light: in its own place it still has weight, and will always fall to meet the surface of the water below it. Consequently if the fire above it were withdrawn, it would not move upward to the surface of the sublunary sphere. And finally, certain peculiar characteristics of fire plainly indicate its superiority over the other three elements. It is of all the most perfectly determinate, the nearest to Form. But this is not surprising, since the body furthest from the centre is also nearest to the most perfect of all natural bodies, that of which the heavens and the heavenly bodies are made.

Of this fifth element and of the nature of the beings whose sole material constituent it is, one can speak only tentatively and with proper reservations; for here observation carries us only a little way. Bodies on this earth show no tendency if left to themselves to move in a circle, but always in a straight line. In the heavens, on the other hand, there is no sign of rectilinear movement: on the contrary, the movements which are most easily analyzed appear to be simple circles described round the earth as centre. Now all movements whatever may be exhaustively divided into the straight, the circular, and the various combinations of these two. Thus the straight and the circular are the only simple or elementary motions. But every natural body has a natural motion, and a simple body has a simple motion. It is therefore reasonable to postulate a fifth simple body endowed with the only remaining simple motion. If there is such a body, it and its motion would clearly enjoy a degree of perfection unattainable by the other elements. Their being is conditioned throughout by contrary oppositions, of qualities (warm — cold, moist — dry) and of places (up — down), and so necessarily exhibits instability and discontinuity. They are therefore in continuous interchange, and at best can only move to their places, where motion is replaced by its contrary rest. But a body endowed with the impulse to circular motion, and set at the circumference of the whole, is in a very different case. Its motion has no contrary: for, though opposition of direction is possible, there can be no opposed termini where there is no terminus at all: and, since this is so, there will also be no contrary opposition of qualities which could afford a basis for change. Instead of moving *to* its place, it will move *in* its place: for perfectly circular movement makes possible for the body as a whole, as no other kind of movement can, at once identity of place and continuity of motion. Hence its movement can be conceived as eternal and unchanging. This postulate, then, gives us precisely the conditions required to account for the unbroken regularity of the observed movements of the stars and for their unchanging order. " For in the whole range of time past, as far as our inherited records reach, no change appears to have taken place either in the whole scheme of the outermost heaven or in any of its proper parts.[17]

We must therefore suppose that the spherical envelope which encloses the world of nature is wholly filled with matter of this kind, in which at intervals, like islands in a sea, the projections which we call the stars are set. However complicated to an observer on the earth the movements of these bodies may appear to be, we must follow Plato's mathematical friend, Eudoxus, in the effort to exhibit these movements as the resultants of a number of combined circular movements. For there can be no forced or unnatural movement where there are no contraries to account for it. The absence of contraries also accounts for the fact that things made of this element escape the senses: for sensation depends on contrary opposition. It is true that men suppose themselves to see the stars; but that cannot be admitted. We conjecture, rather, that these projecting portions of the fifth element disturb by the swiftness of their motion the fire and air below them, so that the air in their neighborhood is ignited. What we see therefore is neither the stars themselves nor fire proper, but the flames incidental to the transformation of air into fire. This is the origin of the heat and light which the heavenly bodies, and particularly the sun, appear to shed upon the earth, with such beneficent results to all things upon it.

The principles already stated involve some important consequences with regard to the individual heavenly bodies. Clearly their existence is as remote from that of the particular things of our experience, as their matter is from the matter of these. A particular man,

Socrates or Coriscus, is born and dies; but these bodies are eternal and unchanging. Each of them is therefore more truly analogous to the species which lives for ever in the succession of passing individuals, than to these individuals themselves. Each of them, and not only they, but each of the concentric spheres which constitute the heavens and create in co-operation its apparent complexity of movement, must be conceived as an individual living substance, which is material and yet not particular. In them, one might say, the union of form and matter attains a degree of perfection which annihilates the opposition of particular and universal.

But the mere presence of matter, however perfectly informed, necessitates, as we have seen, a certain residuary imperfection of which the fact of movement is an indication. And if we attend carefully to the order which the heavens exhibit we shall find it necessary to postulate varying degrees of perfection within it. There is first the outermost region, that of the so-called fixed stars. These stars are observed to return in unchanging order at regular intervals of time to the same positions in the sky; and these appearances are fully accounted for if we suppose that they are all attached to a single revolving sphere. Next come the stars which are called the planets or 'wanderers.' These move generally in the reverse direction, but on paths which in detail are far less easily analyzed. Eudoxus found himself obliged to suppose four distinct motions to account satisfactorily for the observed movements of each of the planets. Lastly, for the Sun and Moon, which are the bodies nearest to the earth, he required three motions in each case. Further study of the matter has shown the necessity of postulating additional motions in every case except that of the fixed stars; and in all, at present, fifty-five spheres seem to be required to account fully for the phenomena of the heavens on the principles laid down. Only eight of these actually have stars attached to them; and no sphere, except that which carries the host of the fixed stars, can have more than one star set in it, since no two planets are equidistant from the centre.[18]

The rationale of the order thus generally described is not easy to detect. But one cannot explain everything; and in a matter of this kind one must be contented with a bare hint of a solution. An arrangement which exhibited a progressive decline in simplicity and perfection of movement in each body, or group of bodies, as they were further from the circumference, would be easily understood. But in the heavens we find complete simplicity in the outer heaven, and the greatest variety of movement in the heavens next to it: for the movements of the sun and the moon are fewer than those of some of the planets. Thus variety of movement is not proportionate to distance from the extremity. A kind of solution offers itself, if we remember that the stars are not inanimate, but things enjoying life and action. "On this view the facts cease to appear surprising. For it is natural that the best-conditioned of all things [God] should have its good without action, that that which is nearest to it [the sphere of the fixed stars] should achieve it by little and simple action, and that which is further removed [the planets] by a complexity of actions, just as with men's bodies one is in good condition without exercise at all, another after a short walk, while another requires running and wrestling and hard training: and there are yet others who however hard they worked themselves could never secure this good, but only some substitute for it. . . . We must then think of the action of the lower stars as similar to that of animals and plants. For on our earth it is man that has the greatest variety of actions. The lower animals have less variety of action than man; and plants perhaps have little action and of one kind only. One thing then has and enjoys the ultimate good, others attain to it, one immediately by few steps, another by many; while yet another does not even attempt to secure it, but is satisfied to reach a point not far removed from that consummation. Thus, taking health as the end, there will be one thing that always possesses health, others that attain to it, one by reducing flesh, another by running and thus reducing flesh, another by taking steps to enable himself to run, thus further increasing the number of movements; while another cannot attain health itself, but only running or reduction of flesh, so that one or other of these is for such a being the end. For while it is clearly best for any being to attain the real end, yet, if that cannot be, the nearer it is to the best the better will be its state. It is for this reason that the earth moves not at all and the bodies near it with few movements. For they do not attain the final end, but only come as near to it as their share in the divine principle permits. But the first heaven finds it immediately with a single movement, and the bodies intermediate between the first and last heavens attain it indeed, but at the cost of a multiplicity of movement." [19]

3. THE ANIMAL KINGDOM [20]

HAVING analyzed, as well as our scanty evidence permits, the eternal order of the heavens, we must now turn to that unstable terrestrial region in which we ourselves live. Here we have abundant information within easy reach, and no pains must be spared to collect it. The loftier interest of the higher study must not be allowed to obscure the importance or the charm of this enquiry. The animal kingdom, from its noblest to its most ignoble members, deserves exhaustive investigation. To the senses, it is true, some animals make no appeal; yet even these delight the philosophic mind, which sees the art with which they are designed and discerns the reasons for each feature. Every work of Nature is wonderful, and, if childish prejudice is put aside, will be found to be beautiful. We repeat, therefore, with a difference, Heraclitus' admonition to those who were shocked at finding the great philosopher in the kitchen. There too, he said, divinities were present. So we say that Nature, even in the least considered of her works, does not move at random, but attains an end and achieves beauty.

The indispensable basis of this achievement is, as we have explained, the constant interchange of the four simple bodies, earth, water, air, and fire; and the order achieved has already been generally characterized as a system of identical forms, eternally repeated in the generation of an endless series of perishing individuals. This order may be further detailed along two main lines. First, we may compare these various forms with one another and study their intricate interrelation within the system. We shall find that, on any principle we can apply, one represents an advance upon another. The single central purpose or form which we call Nature, as it is more perfectly realized in the heavenly bodies than in those of the earth, so on the earth itself finds more adequate fulfilment in one species than another. The line of progression, it is true, is not quite straight and simple. For instance, while animals which have blood are on the whole nobler than those which have not, yet some insects, particularly ants and bees, are the superiors of most sanguineous creatures in intelligence. Nevertheless, taken as a whole, the animal world is found to present a graduated scale of perfection rising to man as its culminating point. Nature proceeds little by little from the lifeless to the animal in such wise that a precise line of demarcation cannot be fixed and doubtful intermediate forms must be recognized. Sponges, for instance, are rooted like plants, but in other respects resemble animals: and the testacean genus as a whole has a certain vegetable character, as contrasted with animals capable of progression. Similarly in the plant world we can detect a continuous scale of ascent towards the animal. The detailed exploration of this graduation is one of the chief ways of determining our conception of Nature.

But there is also another kind of analysis which is essential if the works of Nature are to be understood. We have already observed that the development of a thing is not to be regarded simply as the imposition of form upon matter, but rather as the superimposition of form upon form. The study of natural species shows that the structure of any creature can only be understood as the product of such successive superimpositions. The simple bodies, themselves compositions, as we have seen, of certain elemental contrary forces, are then compounded to make what we may call the *homogeneous* parts of the animal, parts structurally simple, like flesh and bone; and this synthetic effort reaches an initial completeness when the homogeneous parts are put together to form a *heterogeneous* part or organ. But the completeness is only relative: we are at the beginning, not at the end. With this third degree of composition we reach the minimum organism, so little differentiated internally that it is but a single organ. In almost all plants and animals composition proceeds to a fourth stage, in which the organism exhibits a multiplicity of functions and organs. The further stages in the elaboration of nature's handiwork beyond this point cannot be regarded as further degrees of composition; but the elaboration continues, as psychology will show us, to its limit in man. The task which these considerations indicate is an analysis of the animal on lines of structure and function, which will give a precise meaning to such terms as 'higher,' 'lower,' 'nobler,' and the like, by showing the lower as the condition and presupposition of the higher. Man should be seen as taking up into his richer and more complex being every perfection that creatures more poorly endowed succeed in expressing. This analysis is clearly complementary to the extensive study of the species, and can only be pursued with success in conjunction with it.

The principles which should guide us in this enquiry are those already outlined. Form, it has been said, is the unit of being and knowledge. It follows that the change and process which is everywhere manifest in terrestrial phenomena must not be taken as ultimate, but rather as having significance in virtue of that which in it is struggling into existence. It is not the process that makes things what they are: rather it is the determinate nature of the thing that makes and guides the process. Our study, therefore, is not primarily of process and secondarily of the form which it generates, but primarily of the form and secondarily of the process by which in the individual instance it comes into being. We should hope to show that a man has the parts he has because they are necessary conditions of his existence and man is unthinkable without them. Or, if we cannot quite say this, we should hope to see that their presence makes life better for him, directly or indirectly. In any case our starting point will be man as an animal of a certain definite character, and whatever we explain as to his birth and generation will be explained on this basis.

We must also oppose, on the same ground, the tendency, prevalent among our predecessors, to explain organisms by their material composition. It has been supposed, for instance, that the water in the body caused by its currents the formation of the stomach. Apart from the crudity of supposing that water as such is a constituent of the organism, and can create an organ without first creating the homogeneous substance, flesh, such assertions reverse the true relation of form and matter. The operative principle is not matter but form. And though the term 'Nature' is no doubt applied both to the matter and to the form, yet considered as operative in her creatures, whether as motive or as final cause, she must be identified with form and essence.

Now form and essence in the case of things endowed with life is what is called soul. Hence soul is coextensive with life and begins in the plant. In soul, therefore, or at least in that part of it which constitutes the essential character of an animal, is to be found the cardinal principle for the explanation of animal life. Mere body will not make an animal, and no part of the animal can be purely material or purely immaterial. An organism is a system of organs, in which each member serves some partial end and performs some function of value to the whole. As the body comprises and unites the bodily organs, so the soul comprises in a unity the functions of which these are the vehicles; and the body is made for the soul as the member or organ is made for its function. Soul stands for the unity of the functions which at a given stage differentiate the behaviour of living from that of lifeless matter. Its distinguishable features (or 'parts,' as they are often metaphorically termed) are precisely as many as the distinct functions in which it finds expression. It is responsible in animals for birth, growth, reproduction, waking, sleep, progression and all other characteristic functions of animal life. But no final or exhaustive enumeration of these is possible. Comparison of one species with another and analysis of the behaviour of the higher kinds reveals the character of serial graduation already noted which precludes fixed lines of demarcation. The varied life of man is quite easily exhibited as a series of functions (such as nutritive, sensitive, calculative) in which each later term postulates it predecessors as necessary precondition: but to do this is only to single out salient features in a continuous development. Between any two terms intermediate terms can usually be inserted without difficulty. Hence a list of the soul's ' parts ' or functions may be quite reasonably varied according to the context in which it occurs. But the principle at least is clear: the organ is explained by the function, the body by the soul; and, since higher presupposes lower, the soul (that is, the life) of a species is understood with reference to the highest level attained in the mature individual of that species: and soul (that is, life) in general is understood with reference to the highest level which it anywhere attains beneath the moon, that is, with reference to man, and in man by that which is highest in him, namely reason. In saying this we are only asserting once more that form is the only operative principle in being and in knowledge: for the lower is related to the higher as matter to form.

When these principles are fully accepted, and in all living things we see form, as soul, operative on matter, here building success on success, there checked and frustrated, but yet always achieving something with the matter available; when we proceed, as men commonly do, to generalize this operative force as God or Nature, as the totality of the informing activity, triumphing everywhere, though not without difficulty and not always with equal completeness, over the stubborn inertia of matter, it becomes difficult not to fall into picturesque and enthusiastic metaphor. One sees Nature as a cunning craftsman to whom his material is at once limitation and opportunity; who, in the course of his work, turns aside from his main purpose to make use of some little incidental surplus or to convert some flaw into an adornment: or as a painter, who first sketches his outline and then fills in with colour the detail of his picture: or again as a good housekeeper, who allows nothing to be wasted and finds a use for all the leavings of the table. Such metaphors do no harm as long as we remember that this God or Nature is not, like a man, operating upon things from without and forcing upon them a purpose which is not theirs. The word is no doubt used in other senses, but, as we here use it, the nature of a thing is that which it fundamentally is, its form and essence, and, since things are not complete but strive for completion, this form appears as end and the nature becomes a principle of movement. A similar account must be given of the generalized Nature, which will be the form or essence of things natural and their principle of movement — not wholly realized, therefore, in the individuals in which it is embodied, but partly actual, partly potential. And as this Nature is present in anything so far as it attains the perfection of which it is capable, so, comparing one thing with another, we must regard as most natural that thing which is capable of the highest perfection. We may say, then, that man is the most natural of animals because in him animal nature reaches its climax. In him the immanent form reaches the limit of the development possible in the region of birth and decay occupied by the four terrestrial bodies.

It is not possible in this place to pursue the ramifications of Nature, to show how plants bridge the interval between the lifeless and the animal, or to exhibit the bonds which hold the many animal species together and prove their unity. The most widely separated classes can be brought together by analogy. Thus bloodless animals, which have neither blood nor flesh, possess certain features resembling these and serving them as these serve the others. They have also a central organ which takes the place of the heart. Connexions of this kind can be traced everywhere. Besides these there are the wide communities of nature indicated for us by the instinctive wisdom of men, when they marked out great groups comprising a variety of species, such as the Birds and the Fishes. The members of these groups exhibit common attributes, subtly differentiated, however, in each species by the specific nature, since there can be nothing quite identical in creatures specifically distinct. But the best way to illustrate such principles as these for our present purpose is to take the single species of man and state shortly some of the characteristics which mark him out as the culminating point in the scale of animal life.

It is generally recognized that man's great and peculiar gift is his intelligence, the Reason by which he transcends the mere animal and is linked with the Divine. If we study even his bodily structure we shall find sufficient evidence that all is ordered to this as end. Alone among animals man walks erect, thus having his natural parts in their natural position, conformably to the distinction of up and down in the physical universe, and making possible a fuller differentiation of back and front, right and left, than lower animals exhibit. The erect position is facilitated by the diminution of the relative weight and bulk of the upper parts; and this plainly facilitates the motions of the intellect and general sense, which centre in the heart and are obstructed in lower organisms by the bulk and pressure of these parts. The lower animals need two additional feet to carry this weight: their upper parts sink towards the ground; and the head comes to the front. Compared with man they may be regarded as dwarfs, with the upper parts too large and the lower parts too small. Small children show similar characteristics: hence at first they can only crawl, and their intelligence is undeveloped. As we follow the scale of being downwards, we find the feet becoming more numerous and the head closer to the ground, until the animal becomes a plant, destitute of motion and sensation. Its roots are the equivalent of mouth and head; and it may therefore be said to have its upper parts below and its lower parts above.

Standing thus erect, man needs only two feet. Forelegs and forefeet are replaced by arms and hands. These hands were said by Anaxagoras to be the explanation of man's intelligence. But this is the reverse of the truth. Man's intelligence is the explanation of his hands. Considered in themselves hands are at first sight far less effective weapons than many with which lower animals are endowed. It has indeed been argued that man is more poorly equipped than any animal, and least able to guard himself from attack. This would be true if it were not for man's intelligence, which finds in the hand precisely that characteristic of adaptibility to the most varied uses which intelligence needs in its instruments. The hand is not one but many instruments, or perhaps we should say not an instrument at all, but a master key to all instruments whatever. The lion and the eagle cannot change their weapons: man can change his at will. At his choice the hand is talon, hoof, or horn, spear or sword. It is to make possible this variety of use that the fingers are split off from one another, jointed so as to provide a firm and adjustable grip, and the nails reduced to mere protections for the exposed tips of the fingers.

The upright carriage and free-moving upper limbs of man are closely connected with certain superiorities over other animals in the homogeneous parts and their organization. All plants and some lower animals lack unity to such an extent that they continue to live after division. The rising scale in the animal world is the progressive achievement of this unity. Putting on one side the bloodless species, as the less perfect of the two great groups, we find in all other animals a central organ on which all functions depend. This is the heart, the home of the vital heat, the hearth where Nature watches her sacred fire, the citadel of the bodily community. The primary vehicle of this natural heat is the blood, which is developed in the heart and continuously sent forth by it to the furthest limits of the body, so long as life lasts. All the functions of life, therefore, depend in the last resort upon the heart and the blood. In man the heart is hottest and the blood is purest and most abundant. In him and in all the larger animals the heart separates the finer and the thicker blood, sending the former upward, and the latter downward. Now thick warm blood is conducive to strength and thin cool blood to sense perception and thought. This explains the function of the organ next in importance to the heart, the brain. It is not, as some have said, the seat of sensation and thought: it is required rather to cool the blood and by thus tempering its heat to make sensation possible. It is because man is the hottest of animals that his brain is the largest.

A further sign of the superiority of man's material organization is this. It is evident that man has fewer external excrescences than any other animals. He has no horns or talons or beak, no feathers or scales, and little hair. It is true that he has more covering to his head than most animals; but this is needed for the protection of his brain. Hair, horns, and the like are really residual matter, formed from blood not otherwise used up, and of an earthy nature. The smoothness and bareness of the human body may therefore be taken as an indication of the excellence of its economy.

This characteristic is closely connected with man's primacy in the function of sensation. The gift of sensation is universal in the animal world, and serves with the gift of movement, inseparable from it, to mark out the animal from the vegetable. The primary and fundamental sense is touch, which is probably the only sense present in the lowest animals. The fineness and smoothness of the human flesh makes man's sense of touch very much more delicate than that of any other animal. A similar refinement marks the nearly-related sense of taste, as is shown by the softness and breadth of the human tongue and its great freedom of movement. Generally, it may be said that the senses reach their highest perfection in man. For though in all senses except touch and taste he is surpassed by a great number of animals, and may even be said in regard to these other senses, smell, sight and hearing, which operate at a distance, to be the worst equipped for his size of any animal, yet the superiority of these two senses, with the greater power of comparison and estimation which he possesses, give him a subtlety and accuracy of qualitative discrimination which is unrivalled.

Lastly, we must consider the evidence as to man's generation. In the animal world generally, as contrasted with the vegetable, generation depends on the distinction of the sexes. This distinction is a fundamental element in the increased differentiation which the superior unity of the animal necessitates. In the two sexes Nature has explicitly separated for the function of reproduction the two principles of form and matter, activity and passivity. The male contributes nothing material to the offspring: he only provides the impulse which enables the matter offered by the female to attain the determination of which it is capable. This matter may be supposed to be capable by itself of reaching the level of plant life; and if that degree of life were alone required the female would be self-sufficient. Without material combination, by action upon this matter from without, the male principle makes possible to the germ the attainment of the further perfection of sense, which is the constitutive peculiarity or differentia of the animal.

The sex character clearly has an important influence on the whole life of the animal, and the difference between the sexes in their general behaviour is, as one would expect, most marked in man. The difference of function in generation carries with it this consequence. The material, inert, and potential, is in excess, however slightly, in the female as compared with the male: in her there is a relative deficiency in the vital heat, the sign of a relative deficiency in formative energy. Thus form in the female is less dominant over matter than in the male; and though we are bound to recognize the necessity that the female should exist if the species is to be continued, we must yet admit that the female can only exist by a departure from the natural in the sense we have given to that word. This is one of those features of life of which necessity, rather than form, is the explanation.

The subsequent history of the human germ through its stages of embryo, infant, child, adolescent, to maturity, is found on analysis to present a continuous progression from the lowest to the highest levels of life. The unfertilized embryo must be credited, as we have said, with plant life. As it develops it acquires the sense function, which makes it animal; and last of all it puts on those specific characters which give it its peculiar place in the animal world. This process of development is not difficult to conceive as a development of soul correlated with a parallel development of the bodily organs. We have already observed that the bodies of small children show a certain resemblance in the relative weight of the upper parts to those of lower animals of mature age. But that Reason which is man's special gift has no bodily organ: its activity has no connexion with any bodily part. How then can its generation be conceived? Strictly, as incorporeal, it cannot be said to be generated or destroyed at all. With body these attributes must surely vanish. We can only suppose that, in virtue of its divine and timeless nature, it supervenes or enters from without, man's title to membership in a world higher than that in which his life is lived.

4. THE LIFE OF MAN [21]

MAN, like all the rest of Nature, is occupied with the effort to achieve, defend and sustain the form which is the law of his being. He

is the culmination, as we have seen, of the
animal world, and takes up into his fuller being
all the lower levels of life. He is plant in-
verted: he is beast standing erect. The bodily
transformation is the sign of a new life, at
once fulfilling and transcending the lower activities on which it is based. Of this life
thought is the organizing principle; and hence
the account of man's activities is the account
of the operations of human reason.

Reason may be regarded, first, as the fulfilment of the power of apprehension, which,
in the form of sensation, all animals possess.
Beginning with the necessary and fundamental
sense of touch, and, hardly less necessary, the
specialized form of touch which we call taste,
the sense function rises through smell and
hearing to the most valuable of all the senses,
vision. By its range and variety, as well as
by its importance for thinking, vision is clearly
marked out as the master sense. It is true
that touch and taste are more necessary to life:
it is true also that we may be said to learn
more by hearing than by sight — hence the
deaf seem commonly more stupid than the
blind — but this is a secondary consequence of
the use of speech for communication: in its

proper and primary uses sight is plainly the richest and most fruitful of the senses. The higher animals, with man, possess all these five senses; and there is reason to think that with the fifth sense the limit of sensation proper is reached. There are and can be no more senses: the five senses between them make possible the apprehension of every character of bodies that any sense could reveal. Thus so far as mere sensation is concerned the limit of development is reached with the higher animals, and in some of them, as we have already said, the higher senses are more perfect than they are in man.

But sensation is only the first step to knowledge. After we have tabulated the special qualities which each sense reveals, and the other qualities (motion, rest, size, shape, number) which they combine to reveal, we are still a long way from the wisdom of man. A number of further gifts are required, possessed by few if any other animals, before thought becomes possible. Sensation is in itself but a momentary affection. The first necessity is that the results of this affection shall be seized and retained by the organism. And what begins in lower creatures as a mere persistence of the sense presentation after the stimulus is withdrawn, gradually wins a degree of freedom from the stimulus and develops into memory and imagination. Finally, when memories of like things combine and organize themselves into experience, we have the nearest approach to knowledge which is possible without conscious and deliberate effort of thought. The stages of this development are hard to determine, and the process is most easily described by metaphors. All starts of course from sensation, and the deliverance of sense may be said to be in motion as contrasted with the immobility of the known universal. So one may liken the process to the rallying of an army in flight. Here and there a soldier stands his ground: about him others gather: and in a short time the unrelated units have become one body amenable to command. So the swift sensations pause and group themselves to form the rudimentary universals which are the germ of knowledge.

Knowledge is first pursued as instrumental to action and production: it is only by degrees that it comes to win its freedom, when the primary needs have been met and sufficient recreation provided, perhaps with the aid of a class, like the priests of Egypt, freed from economic ties and set apart in leisure for this work. Now in the field of production experience means the ability to deal with particular situations of a certain kind as they arise. He who is a craftsman and nothing more has reached just this point. He knows, in a sense, the thing to do; but he cannot explain what he does to another, nor teach another to do it otherwise than by encouraging imitation. It is not till experience turns into art that we are really justified in using the term knowledge in connexion with production. The architect and the physician have experience, and it is their business always to deal with particular situations: they cannot build or heal in general or universally: but they have also knowledge of the universal, health or house, which is the explanation of every step they take because it is the fixed goal of their efforts. This knowledge is what we call art, and its possession makes possible teaching properly so-called. It is the knowledge of a form, arising out of and expressing itself in repeated efforts to create or restore this form. It is valued no doubt mainly for what it produces, yet also from the first to some extent on its own account. The wise

man who heals or builds is no mere utility.
Further, as productive thought passes from
necessities to luxuries, the very fact that utility
is left behind confers on such pure delights as
those of music and poetry a higher dignity.
Last of all, even pleasure is left behind, and
thought is permitted to fulfil its own nature
without external control or limitation, freed
finally from the tyranny of particulars, explor-
ing the universal forms and reasons of things,
and thus satisfying the impulse which makes
the mere exercise of the sense of sight, quite
apart from anything that may come from it, a
delight to man.

In the second place, Reason is the fulfilment
of the power of free movement which is the
other chief distinctive gift of animal life. We
have said that no animal wholly lacks sensation, and where there is sensation there is also
appetite. This, the lowest form of the motive
power, must therefore be credited to all animals; and on it is superimposed in some of
the higher animals anger, and in man, besides
anger, a yet more complex motivation which
may be called desire; this represents the limit
of the possible development of this vital power.
The development on the volitional or motive

side goes hand in hand with the development in the power of apprehension, for apprehension is a precondition of all animal movement. The movement of appetite requires only the sense-perception of an appropriate physical object. The cow, for instance, senses the grass and eats; and in man, however overlaid with judgement and calculation it may be, the same process is still recognizable. Anger clearly presupposes in a higher degree than appetite independence of presented fact, but the situation is still the dominant factor. Desire brings a new freedom, presupposing a developed intelligence, in which the possibilities of a situation are exploited for the achievement of good or the prevention of evil, in which therefore for the first time we can speak of purpose and intention. Every movement of desire has a good for its goal. The good is the end desired, and the desire springs from man's nature as he looks out on the world, having a continuous existence independent of opportunity for its realization. The perception of such opportunity is the product of successful deliberation, in which thought at the bidding of desire seeks for means by which the given end may be helped into existence. Every movement of desire is thus an attempt to achieve a good by appropriate means. The distinction of chosen means and desired end is the peculiar mark of human conduct, in which animal movement reaches its final goal.

In the light of these considerations it is not difficult to discern the outlines of the problem of conduct. We have only to recall the point already made that each human being in his continuous development from the infant to the grown man is ascending the scale of being and thus building or unfolding by degrees his human nature. The firm purpose which is truly said to be more natural to man than the explosive vacillations of appetite and anger is for that very reason not a gift from Nature, inborn like sight or hearing, but an achievement hard won and strenuously sustained by means of effort inspired by love of the form which it both is and seeks. And the effort may be painful: for here as elsewhere matter is apt to show itself recalcitrant. The animal nature, which is destined in man to be overcome by a higher principle, and to find in that submission its final satisfaction, submits nevertheless often with difficulty and after a struggle in which the victory is not always on one side.

In the interest of the form which is to be, these tendencies have to be moderated and harmonized, as a painter mixes and measures the tones and colours with which he would achieve beauty. And as the colours so mixed and measured are in a sense themselves the beauty achieved, so these ordered and disciplined impulses are no mere means to something beyond, but themselves the good or end, their own justification.

This, then, is the problem of conduct on one side. Its solution is goodness of character, an established discipline which is in love with itself and continuously achieves its own reproduction through every change of circumstance. This achievement is its consistent purpose, the ruling consideration to which all others — of pleasure, wealth, honour, or the most precious results of man's productive skill — are strictly subordinated: it is itself the happiness which men are said to seek; for it is welcomed for itself and never for anything it may bring with it, while it is independent, so far as the human can be, of the favour of man and circumstance. The various facets of this disciplined character are the familiar virtues — courage, temperance, generosity and the rest — each of which stands for its happy mastery over a particular kind of emotion or situation. Before turning to the other side of the ethical problem, it will be best to determine rather more precisely the features of this discipline which character, as manifested in action, is intended to attain.

The colours which the painter uses are not in themselves either beautiful or ugly, if beauty is taken to stand for success, ugliness for failure, in the art: it is only in composition that they acquire these attributes. The same could be said of the different kinds of food or exercise between which the trainer or physician chooses in prescribing for his client: each has different attributes which make it suitable to one place, time, and situation, unsuitable to another. Further, in every such case the amount is all-important: it would be of little use to prescribe a given food or exercise without saying how much of it was to be taken. The right ingredient may be used, but if it exceeds or falls short of the due quantity it will bring failure to the extent of its excess or defect; sickness will result instead of health, weakness instead of strength, ugliness instead of beauty. Here then we seem to have a general law of human production, that success depends on a quantitative adjustment of materials with reference to time, place, and situation; that the product as a whole attains its characteristic perfection so far as each ingredient avoids excess and defect and exhibits a neutral or mean quantity.

It is this Law of the Mean that is the secret of the virtuous discipline. The goodness which man achieves in himself is of course no more a quantity than the health or beauty he creates in other things: but this achievement, like that creation, depends on a quantitative adjustment by means of which things themselves indifferent come to exhibit in combination the desired quality. The elements to be adjusted are those powers of action and emotion which belong to man's natural endowment. Emotions like appetite, anger, envy, pity, love, hatred, actions like running, walking, speaking, singing are themselves neither good nor bad. But it is not something other than these that makes the difference between the good and bad man: it is these themselves in their permutations and combinations, by the presence of each at the right place and time in the right or mean degree. Thus courage is a quantitative rightness in respect of two opposed emotions which dangerous situations tend in the normal man to arouse: let us call them fear and cheer. Either emotion in excess will throw a man off his balance and make him do foolish or even disgraceful things: in proportion to their defect he will be cold, phlegmatic, inactive. With both in due measure he will be at once cautious and enterprising; his distaste for danger will be balanced by the excitement of resourceful improvisation; and even if disaster comes he will still enjoy the mastery of self which enables him to hold in spite of all to his great purpose, to make the most of that which he has it in him to be.

The excitements in which Temperance is shown are those of the appetites which man shares with the animals. Here again it is no mere abstinence or suppression that is demanded. It is true that the temperate man will despise pleasures which many would value, that he will forgo with equanimity pleasures which few men would forgo without pain, but he will retain the appetite for all necessary and healthy pleasures and welcome its satisfaction where no higher interest suffers incidental damage.

Character is also thought to be specially tested in the control of anger, in the use of wealth whether great or small, in the attitude to honours, offices, and other forms of public recognition; and private life calls for social gifts in which every self-respecting man will strive to be proficient. If we examined each case in detail we should find everywhere operative the Law of the Mean, everywhere an impulse normal to human nature and in itself innocent, but qualified as bad or good by the degree of its presence in given circumstances. We should also find each virtue opposed not by a single vice, but by two possible developments of character, a habit of excess and a habit of defect, each faulty, though never to the same extent. Thus cowardice (the habit of excess in fear) and licence (the habit of excess in appetite) are faults to which human nature is prone; but the other extremes, defect of fear and insensibility to the pleasures of appetite, are much more uncommon, especially the latter, and seem hardly to deserve so harsh a name as vice. Indeed the fearless man will pass for brave and the frigid for temperate. But in truth virtue is always a gift for the mean, not only because like art it lives by achieving a mean quantity in that which is its vehicle, but also because, unlike art, it stands between two faults, on the razor's edge which divides them.

Since it is often a help to the mind when a theory is given concrete embodiment, we may, adopting a rather more external point of view, find in the Greek notion of magnanimity a kind of picture of the correct attitude to life. The magnanimous man is justly convinced of his own great worth, avoiding on the one hand the vanity of those who think too much, and on the other the weakness of those who think too little of their capacities. He is proficient in every virtue, and values above all else that proficiency. Scrupulous on this account in small things as in great, he yet cares little for what man or circumstance may bring him. Great honours from good men will give him pleasure, moderated, however, by the reflection that virtue in him is only receiving its deserts, or at least that this is the best men have to offer it. Of honours otherwise he will take no account. By the vicissitudes of fortune he will be little moved. He will not court danger or go into it on slight provocation, but in a great cause he will be prodigal of his life, which he knows can be bought too dear. Ready to give, but ashamed to receive benefits (since the receiver is in the inferior position), he will always reply to a service with one greater. Similarly, he will seldom or never ask for help, but will readily offer it; and while he will be great among the great, he will be unpretending in the company of lesser folk. He will not compete for places of honour or go where others come first. He will indeed seem lazy and dilatory except where great honour or great issues are at stake, a doer of few things but those great and notable. He is always frank and open in his dealings, both with friends and enemies. He is little given to admiration, forgetful of injury received, reluctant to speak about his fellows either in praise or blame, and very difficult to provoke into complaint about small necessities or comforts, as one who cares more for beauty and distinction in things than for profit and use. His bodily movements will be slow, his voice deep, and his speech measured: for a shrill voice and hurried movements are the signs of an excitement to which scarcely anything could move him. In the magnanimous man character thus acquires a grace and elegance which justifies us in calling him the ornament of the virtues.

But the problem of conduct is still far from completely stated. We have throughout presumed the coöperation of intelligence, but we have said nothing precise as to the nature or conditions of the coöperation. We have spoken of a purpose developed out of a desire for good by means of an intellectual activity called deliberation; we have described discipline of character as achieved by a regulation of appetite and emotion analogous to the harmonious adjustment of diverse ingredients on which depends the success of man's productive activities. The good desired, we have said, is the continuous reproduction in action of the form which is goodness; and this form must clearly be the controlling principle of the required regulation of the emotional nature. But how can this form operate without being known? It is plain that we credit man as productive with knowledge of the form which he proposes to create. The physician is not properly equipped without a knowledge of health — first of health in general, secondly of health in reference to the peculiarities of the particular patient under treatment; and the

[95]

architect's general knowledge of house-con-struction must be particularized into the con-ceived plan of a house, fully detailed as to situation, measurements, and material, before he begins to build. Is not such general and special knowledge also necessary in the field of conduct? Can a man achieve goodness un-less he knows at the start, first, what goodness in general is, secondly, the special requirements of his particular case, and is thus enabled to guide the development with foreknowledge of its issue?

It is not surprising that such hints and analogies have led men to include Wisdom among the cardinal virtues, or even to go fur-ther and assert, with Socrates, that all virtue is summed up in this word. Like many para-doxes, this view conceals a truth, as we shall see; but we must first make an important distinction. The words ' wise ' and ' wisdom ' are applied over the whole field of knowledge, and they are most properly applied to the purest knowledge, which is that of the highest being. Of such being we have already said that it does not change or move but is time-lessly what it is. The knowledge of it, there-fore, cannot be either sought or required for action or production. Action and production are concerned always with that which can be changed, and have existence only in changing it. In fact each kind of production requires a special knowledge, and the knowledge required for action is also a specialized knowledge different from any of these. The knowledge required is in every case that of the form to be produced or achieved. Before considering, therefore, whether and in what sense perfect action springs from wisdom, we can be sure of this that it does not spring from wisdom in general, nor even from the highest kind of wisdom; but, if at all, from a special practical wisdom, which is at bottom a knowledge of man; and man, as we have seen, is not even the highest achievement of nature. Wisdom in the knowledge of the higher realms of being is of course also to some extent attainable by man, and may also claim the name of virtue, but since it is not attained and expressed in action, the question of its place in life must be postponed. To avoid confusion, then, let us reserve the name of Wisdom for this, and call the intellectual attribute which is our immediate concern, Prudence or Judgement.

The suggestion then is that the development of character sketched above is made possible by a perfection of the intelligence in its practical use, which gives a man knowledge of the 'form to be achieved, similar to the knowledge of health which the physician possesses, and must therefore be regarded as the virtue of virtues. This perfection will be Prudence or Judgement. The suggestion cannot be accepted as it stands. It is true that these terms, Prudence and Judgement, may well be applied to a practical gift not rare in our experience. The judgement which unravels a particular problem of conduct with an immediate certainty needing no support from argumentation, the gift of moral policy which enables a statesman through all his decisions to keep a firm hold of man's highest needs and interests, these, and others such as these, are the well attested fruits of man's practical intelligence. But experience leaves us in no doubt that they are found in the old, not in the young, and are the fruit, not the seed, of a disciplined character.

We have to remember that the parallel between the activities of action and production fails at a point which is here all-important.

The matter to be informed by artist or craftsman has an independent existence: he operates upon it from without: but the agent is at work in conduct and character upon character and conduct. We cannot plausibly bisect him into an agent and a patient, an intelligence which acts and an unreason which is acted on; nor can we suppose him to accept as intelligent a form which as emotional and unintelligent he refuses. Intelligence in itself is not as a matter of fact active. If it were, the problems of conduct would be like those of mathematics, and the small boy could be presented by his teachers with the principles of all solutions. A practical problem is a problem set by desire or some other impulse, and Judgement, the gift of the practical intelligence, is address in the solution of the problems set by the desire for the form which is the human good. It is only so far as this desire effectively exists that the intellectual problems incidental to its satisfaction become practical problems; and it is only so far as the more primitive appetites and emotions accept order and measure that the desire for the good achieves effective existence. It is impossible, therefore, to conceive the progress of the individual towards virtue as a development controlled by fore-knowledge of its issue.

Both observation and general principles already laid down enforce upon us the view that intelligence, which is man's highest gift, is the last to achieve its perfection, and can achieve it only in the degree in which the lower activities on which it supervenes succeed in achieving theirs. And while this must be true of intelligence in general, it has especial point in the field of action, where it is not merely a true assertion that is required but a true assertion backed by a right desire. The characteristic proposition of the practical intelligence is the proposition implicit in every purpose that the action is good or worth doing. This kind of proposition is not one which mere thought and discussion will establish. The philosopher can do little in this field to harmonize differences of opinion: for differences of opinion are at bottom differences of character, and thought of this kind is generated by conduct rather than conduct by thought. Hence the young and those whose character is undeveloped, though in the field of pure thought, in mathematics, for instance, they may have reached a high degree of proficiency, are not yet fit students of the problem of conduct.[22] They live by impulse and lack the necessary basis in character which will give the discussion actuality. On the other hand many possess the fundamental truths, latent in character and conduct, long before they actually think them, if they ever distinctly think them at all.

It is only in this sense true that Prudence or Judgement is the summary of all virtue. The character built up and established by right action, assisted by the example of others, by public opinion, by the collective wisdom of society as embodied in law and constitution, brings with it, as it reaches its own perfection, the knowledge of the good achieved and the ability to perceive the means to its maintenance and repetition. The due regulation of action and emotion generates in the end a consciousness of the system which is its explanation and justification. Judgement is thus the sum of all the virtues in the sense that all the virtues of character are needed to make its existence possible, and in it find their common fulfilment.

Action, however, is not the whole of man's life. His intelligence has other tasks nobler than those of conduct, though it has none more urgently necessary. Proficiency in these tasks we have called Wisdom, and we must conclude this account of the human good with an attempt to explain its importance.

All pleasure and happiness whatever springs from one source, from the exercise of capacity, from being what Nature meant one to be. It is not rest but activity that brings pleasure: and while the unobstructed exercise of any natural gift on its appropriate object is pleasant, the greatest pleasure will be found in the exercise of the highest gift on the most perfect object within its competence. The highest gift of man is reason, and this is most itself when it has won freedom from the importunities of daily life and action, and contemplates, with no external interest but as a mere spectator, the eternal order of the real. In such activity man transcends some of his human limitations and approximates his life to the divine. Philosophic thought, while it lasts, has a continuity and self-sufficiency which is in sharp contrast with the abrupt transitions and interruptions of the practical life: man is for the time independent of external circumstances, even of his body and its changes. The poet [23] advised mortal man to think of human and mortal things; but he was wrong. Man can and should indulge the immortal in him, and imitate as far as he can, though of necessity intermittently, the life of the immortal gods. The Reason which has no bodily organ, which is active without change or movement of any bodily part, is in its own proper use only negatively conditioned by the ordering of appetite and emotion in which the perfection of conduct consists. To that perfection it owes its freedom. Wisdom, the ability to use this freedom, is man's final achievement and crowning virtue.

5. THE CITY [24]

OUR account of man's life could not claim even the completeness of an outline if it did not include some account of the City and some explanation of its importance in man's development.

There is a common inclination to regard the forms of society as somewhat arbitrary accretions upon human life, inventions of man's mind and will, which man having made can undo or do without, and thus as opposed to nature, which man is powerless to alter. This view is fundamentally wrong. All men are endowed by nature with the impulse to association, and this impulse finds its full and final completion in the life of the city. Men may therefore be said to be by nature citizens. Historically the city is not the first expression of this impulse. First comes the association of the sexes for the procreation and rearing of children, leading to the organization of the household for the supply of man's daily needs. Households group themselves into villages; and finally the villages, seeking a better and fuller life, consent to be united and absorbed in a wider unity of which the visible symbol is the walled city with its temples, law-courts and market places. First life, then more and better life: that is the law of man's development; and with the city that development is completed, not indeed in the sense that man as citizen is all he might be, but in the sense that the best is now for the first time within his reach. No element in the good life is wholly lacking: the City-State is a sufficient field for the exercise of every gift and power of man.

Man then is naturally a citizen. Even if he had nothing to gain from the City as a market, or in other tangible ways, he would still seek it for his own satisfaction. For such is man's nature, and those who do not need a city (if there are any) are either too high or too low to be counted men. If they are not gods, they are in love with war, and choose to be brigands and outcasts.

But the City does of course take up into itself the purposes of the lesser and more primitive associations on which it supervenes, in order to carry them to further issues. It does help to the procreation and education of children and to the provision of the necessaries of life. If it did not, it could not claim to embrace and complete the household and the village. The City is therefore much more than a mere alliance or voluntary association of households or villages for the purpose of satisfying certain further needs which these institutions were not able to supply or supplied inadequately. It may have originated, as Greek tradition says, in a local unification of scattered villages; and the immediate advantages which it offered may have been additional facilities for the exchange of goods and increased security against crime and violence. And these three are still, and will always remain, essential conditions of city life. But these alone do not make a city, which is the association in good living of families and clans for the sake of a complete and self-sufficient life.

It follows that the task of government is not that of mere correlation on the one hand nor on the other a mere facilitation of exchange, with provision for the settlement of disputes as they arise and for the punctual detection and punishment of crime and violence. The task is far more comprehensive. The care of a city must be its happiness, and its happiness depends upon its virtue — a sufficiency of wealth and material equipment being presupposed — and the happiness and virtue of a city is the happiness and virtue of its citizens. This fundamental aim transforms what would otherwise be a convenient temporary alliance into a partnership in good living, and turns law from mere articles of association into principles of life and safeguards of happiness. Ultimately the city's only justification is the noble deeds of its members, and no act of government can claim to be judged by any other test than this.

It is therefore nothing less than the obligation to a certain manner of life that the City lays upon its members. This life is laid down in general outline in the constitution, developed in further detail by the laws, which are then applied to the changing needs of the day in the decrees and other executive acts of the government. The constitution is thus all-important, and it is not surprising that some cities trace their constitution to a divine or divinely inspired source. On the formal or legal side the constitution is the instrument which establishes the various magistracies and other authorities within the city, defining their several functions and mutual relations; and the varieties of constitution are rightly held to depend on the various definitions given to the supreme authority. Thus in a monarchy one is supreme, in an oligarchy few, and in a democracy the whole citizen body. From this point of view, in short, the constitution is regarded as essentially the specification of the government of the city. But it is only a very abstract view of the facts that can be content to see no further than this. The determination of the government is the ordering of a living body, the imposition of form on appropriate matter; and, considered from this wider point of view, the constitution can be seen to carry the full significance claimed for it above as the determination in principle of the life of the citizen.

If this more concrete view of the constitution is adopted, the legal forms of government are seen to be sometimes even a misleading guide to the character of a city. An undemocratic constitution may be administered democratically, and a democratic constitution may cloak oligarchic principles. But such a state of things must be unstable, and will not as a rule last long. It occurs most often when the constitution has been changed, and indicates that the change has been imperfectly assimilated or that the authors of the change misjudged the facts. For a constitution is a record of facts as well as a precept of conduct. The distribution of power between the various sections of the population is not variable at the will of the legislator, nor can a constitution create a love of virtue or a preference for peace over war in citizens whose every thought and act implies a love of war or a preference for wealth over virtue. Law can do much no doubt, especially with the young, but the legislator is limited, like every artist, by his material, and is always to some extent merely expressing and endorsing the actual preferences of the men for whom he legislates, and the actual relations between classes and other constitutive elements.

It is obvious, then, that the framer of a constitution has before him a much more profound and complicated question than a consideration of the different forms of government would at first sight suggest. His decision can be no abstract preference for the rule of one or of a few or of the multitude. Human nature is of course at bottom one and the same, and there is therefore one ideal for all men and for every city. The question, ' what is the best life? ' is capable of a definite answer, and consequently there is one form of city which is always and everywhere the best. The innermost character of the city is expressed by its constitution, which preserves the city's identity through all changes of its human material, and guarantees the continual reproduction from day to day of the same ordered life. Therefore the first necessity for the legislator is to know what this best life is. But in fact men and conditions vary. Different groups of men will seek happiness under different forms and by different means, and all are restricted to the means available. The legislator will require to study the population committed to his charge and the conditions under which they live. Are they equal or unequal in wealth, in virtue, in knowledge? Are they pastoral or agricultural or mercantile or seafaring, and in what proportions? Is the city by the sea or near the sea, and has it a port, or is it inland? Only after answering these and other similar questions will the legislator be able to say, from his knowledge of the best life and the best form of constitution, how this people can come nearest to these. His decision will be a constitution, in form a determination of the government, but in fact the recommendation of a way of life, firmly based, if he is successful, on existing facts and bringing out all their hidden possibilities of strength and goodness.

When the constitution is made, a primary requisite in every official or magistrate in the city is absolute loyalty to the constitution, that is, complete acceptance of the ideal implicit in it. This is necessary not only in the magistrate but also in every citizen; and loyalty to the constitution is shown not only in a citizen's public acts, but also in private life and in actions which may appear to have no direct reference to the politically organized community. Private life is often the source of political disturbances. Perhaps there ought to be a special magistracy whose duty it should be to watch for and check ways of living which are not in harmony with the spirit of the constitution. But prevention is better than cure. Hence the city's clearest duty and opportunity is with the young. The city must take the responsibility of seeing by the regulation of marriage and childbirth that its future members are born in fit conditions, so that even the bodies of babies may respond to the aims of the legislator. It is even more obvious that education cannot safely be left, as most Greek cities leave it, in private hands. How shall the citizen be moulded to suit the city and learn to do those acts which express and preserve its special character, if every father looks after his own children and teaches them, or has them taught, whatever he thinks fit? Laws will be of little effect unless the citizens have assimilated the spirit of the constitution, and this condition is not likely to be satisfied unless education is made the city's care and the same for all. It is the special distinction of Sparta that she, almost alone among Greek cities, has recognized and acted upon this truth.

It is conceivable that a community might exist which was satisfied to dispense with laws and to entrust its fortunes to a single man, preëminent in ability, leaving him entirely free to decide what was best and adapt conduct to circumstance. It may even be argued that, given sufficient eminence and wisdom in the ruler, such an arrangement has by its flexibility an important advantage over any other. But the condition is hard to fulfil, and, even supposing it fulfilled, the size of cities makes the task of such a ruler almost superhumanly difficult. Other practical difficulties are easily seen. In general, therefore, it may be said that good government is government according to Law, and that it is only through Law that the constitution finds expression and effect. A law is a general rule governing the behaviour of citizens, backed by force sufficient to ensure observance. Its merits depend on its adequacy to express and maintain the spirit of the constitution, and therefore a law which would be good, for instance, in an oligarchy may be bad in a democracy. Magistrates and officials are essentially only guardians and ministers of law, from which they derive the authority for their acts. In a well-governed city, in short, law rules, and the rule of law is clearly preferable to the rule of man. It may be objected that law, being general, will break down in unforeseen cases and cannot adapt itself to circumstances. But the city will have officers specially trained in applying the general rules to particular cases, and appeal is allowed from the written law, when the latter fails, to the spirit of law embodied in the immemorial tradition of human wisdom. Further, man is not pure reason: he is half beast, and even in the wisest judgement is apt to be disturbed by passion. Law gives a strong safeguard against the whims and passions of the day, and may be described as reason unaffected by desire. For these reasons there is nothing more important to the city than a law-abiding spirit in the citizens. The spirit of obedience to law must be jealously maintained, especially in small things in which non-compliance passes most easily unobserved. For where law has no authority there is no constitution. Law, fully and loyally enforced and observed, is in practice the only means by which the end proposed in the constitution is capable of attainment.

If we turn now from these general principles to the existing varieties of constitution, we find that the main controversy concerns the question, in whom should the guardianship of law and the control of the executive officers of the city be vested. In effect we are usually offered a choice between two alternatives. The partisans of oligarchy plead for a select body of persons eminent by reason of their wealth or of their ability or of the combination of these factors. The partisans of democracy, on the other hand, urge that the whole body of free citizens should retain the general control of its own destiny. Both claims seem to some extent justified. It is hard to resist the claims of virtue; and wealth, though too often overvalued, as at Carthage and even at Sparta, is undoubtedly an element of value in the life of the city. It seems fair that those who contribute more, whether of wealth or of virtue, should have a greater share, when power and authority are distributed, than those who contribute less. Yet there seems also to be danger of a fallacy. If men are unequal in one respect, are they to be made unequal in every

[114]

other? The democrat, on the other hand, may be accused of the opposite fallacy. All men born free, he sees, are so far equal; and from equality in this one attribute he is ready to conclude a universal equality of citizens which is only properly recognized when the highest officers of the city are selected not by merit but by the chance of the lot. Yet his case also has its strong points. It may well be that when many meet together they attain collectively a wisdom and sureness of judgement beyond the reach of any individual among them, that their strength and not their weakness is summed, that they agree by what they have of reason and, differing in their passions and desires, are thus collectively misled and seduced with more difficulty than even the best of men is. Their collective wealth also exceeds that of any individual. And if these arguments are rejected, it may still be urged that it is the whole mass of the free citizens after all that the laws deal with, and that ruling is one of those arts in which the consumer is the best judge of failure and success.

Each claim then has some justification, though each can be pushed to absurdity. The question how far either can be honoured must, however, be influenced by certain further considerations. In the first place, we assume that in all true governments the rulers have in mind the welfare of the city as a whole. If they consider only their own private or sectional interests, they are not governing and there is no genuine constitution. Such abeyance or perversion of government may well be least harmful, as Plato thought, when it assumes the democratic form. But this consideration is not strictly relevant to the determination of the question before us. Secondly, the point already made has to be remembered, that much depends on the nature and occupations of the population for which the constitution is intended. The reason why there is a variety of constitutions is that every city contains a variety of elements which may be differently proportioned and combined. There are riches and poverty and moderate means, differently distributed in different localities. Thirdly, considering these differences, it is evident that the chances of good and stable government will be greatly increased if the middle position preponderates over the two extremes. Both riches and poverty are seen in fact to conduce to weakness and crime: reason consorts best with moderate means. Further, friendship and comradeship flourish most among equals, and for this reason a city should be composed, as far as possible, of equals; but this equality can only be found in the middle position. It is also clearly shown by experience that moderate means make men contented and peaceful and averse to rash experiment, free from the arrogance of the rich and the envy of the poor. It would be best then if all citizens were moderately endowed, or, if that is not possible, the middle class should at least be the largest of the three classes.

If we consider the opposition of democracy and oligarchy with these points in mind, we shall see no reason to doubt that in any normal city it will be possible to frame a constitution which will do substantial justice to both pleas and by mixing the two principles produce an arrangement better and stronger than either. Under one set of conditions it will approximate more to the oligarchic, under others to the democratic type; but always the one-sidedness of both these types will be avoided. The claims of virtue, of wealth, and of free-birth will all be recognized in some measure, and the middle class will be given the opportunity of playing its natural part as makeweight and mediator between rich and poor. In order to effect this it will only be necessary to secure for the magistrates greater independence than democracies allow them, and to exclude from certain functions of government those who do not satisfy a moderate property qualification.

In the old days such a constitution as this was often called a democracy; but modern democracy has become government by the poor in their own interest. Magistrates are multiplied, and their tenure of office shortened. The mass-meeting of citizens keeps all authority in its own hands and continually over-rides the law by its decrees. The result is that respect for law vanishes from the city, and liberty gives place to licence. Such a state of things is not government but anarchy. Instead of prescribing to all its members a rule of life and an ideal of virtue, the city lets each go his own way and trusts to chance for the result. Democracy in this extreme form is thus the refusal on the part of the community to fulfil its primary duty, the care of the happiness of its members. But freedom and equality do not mean doing as one pleases, and submission to the constitution is not slavery but salvation.

III. EPILOGUE

ARISTOTELIANISM [25]

TWO things may be said of Aristotle which can be said perhaps of all really great thinkers: first, that he summed with finality the thought of an age, and, secondly, that his age did not understand his message.

There is a story [26] that Theophrastus, Aristotle's successor at the Lyceum, who died about 287 B.C., left his own and Aristotle's books to his pupil Neleus, who took them away with him to Scepsis in the Troad. It is said that Neleus' heirs, fearing the book-collecting propensities of the Attalid kings, concealed the manuscripts in a cellar, where they remained for more than 150 years, until, in or about the year 100 B.C., they were bought and restored to Athens by a certain Apellicon of Teos. Of this story, which is not inherently very credible and is told with rather damaging variations in the few passages in which it occurs, various explanations are offered. It seems incredible that the wise and learned Theophrastus, one of the few among Aristotle's successors at the Lyceum who were capable both of understanding the master's teaching and of continuing his work, should have alienated from the school by will the sole existing copies of his writings. In fact, Theophrastus' successor Straton seems to have continued not unworthily the Aristotelian tradition, and to have grappled with metaphysical problems in a fashion which presupposes knowledge and study of Aristotle's most difficult works. In his successors, however, it is difficult to detect any signs of metaphysical or serious philosophical speculation. For nearly two hundred years an Ethic directed merely to edification, and a Rhetoric designed as a weapon for the competition of practical life, with some efforts in literary and philosophical history, exhaust the energies of the school. To the educated reader Aristotle seems to be represented only by the much praised Dialogues.[27]

The suggestion has at least some plausibility that the story of the cellar in the Troad is merely a picturesque rendering of the failure of the Aristotelian impulse in the school he founded. To say that they lost the master's works is only another way of saying that they ceased to study them. In any case there is little room for doubt as to the historical fact that during the first century B.C., under Andronicus of Rhodes, the works were re-ordered and edited, and the study of them was seriously undertaken. But the Aristotelian impulse was dead beyond hope of revival. The school now saw not so much a world of thought to conquer as a body of doctrine to digest and expound. Commentary, always patient and sometimes profound, was the best offering they could make to the memory of their master. A great man, we are told, lays on the world the duty of understanding him. In the case of Aristotle it proved a heavy burden. No great thinker has occasioned such masses of comment, instructed and uninstructed, good, bad, and indifferent; and none has given in proportion so little of direct inspiration to original thought.

It was only by slow degrees that Aristotle climbed to the proud mediaeval pinnacle registered by Dante in his celebrated phrase " the master of them that know." His works — or at least his most profound and important works

— were neglected, as we have said, for two centuries after his death. The revival of Aristotelian study under Andronicus had no doubt some effect; but among the learned of the Graeco-Roman world there can have been few at any time who perceived his greatness. The more recent and less metaphysical speculations of Stoics, Epicureans, and Sceptics offered at first more living issues, and the Eclectics and Neo-Platonists of subsequent generations merely restored Aristotle to an honoured place among the great teachers of the past. In popular estimation, it may be conjectured, not merely Plato (who still stands by his side today), but Heraclitus, Pythagoras, Democritus, Zeno of Citium and Epicurus of Samos, with the encyclopaedic Posidonius and many less known names, stood as high or higher than Aristotle. There is little evidence that the Romans seriously studied any works of Aristotle, apart from the published dialogues, except the *Rhetoric* and the *Poetics*. It was not perhaps till the fourth century A.D. that the logical works, afterwards so preponderant in the Aristotelian tradition, began to receive general attention. St. Augustine as a young man read the *Categories,* and the *Analytics*

were translated by the Roman senator Vettius
Agorius about the same time.

Meanwhile the commentators of Athens were
annotating all the master's works. The
splendid edition of the Greek commentaries
on Aristotle which the modern world owes
to the learning and enterprise of the Berlin
Academy comprises twenty-three large octavo
volumes, the surviving product for the most
part of this immense activity. All but a few of
the works here printed were written between
200 and 550 A.D. on an identical plan. Sentence by sentence the words of 'the philosopher' are explained, their place in his argument determined, their references to the past
elucidated; and from time to time a long di-
gression opens the way to a wider treatment
of a matter of special interest. By general
consent the greatest of these commentators
is Alexander of Aphrodisias (c. 200 A.D.),
to whom Aristotelian scholarship owes a still
accumulating debt. Some of the others are
mainly prized for the light they throw on
the text or on the history of Greek thought.
But even as expositors the greater number still
have their value. They were not isolated en-
quirers, but exponents of a great tradition.

The Athenian schools of philosophy were suppressed by Justinian in 529 A.D. Some of the dispossessed professors took refuge in Persia under the protection of King Chosroes, and by his aid after a short time they secured the permission of the emperor to settle at Alexandria. But pagan philosophy did not much flourish there, and it was not from Alexandria that the West was destined to receive the torch of ancient learning. The Greek tradition made its home next in Constantinople; and there the work of expounding the Aristotelian philosophy was continued without a break for many centuries. From Constantinople the study of Aristotle spread among the Syrians. Syriac commentaries existed as early as the middle of the fifth century, and continued to be produced as late as the twelfth century. From this source, by a strange freak of history, the learning of Western Europe was to receive renewal and reform.

The nations of Western Europe were of course primarily the heirs of Rome and the Western Empire. The Greek language was not included in their inheritance. The great Greeks could be known at most at second hand; and Aristotle was so little read in im-

perial Rome, that he could not be expected to
figure prominently in its legacy. But Aristotle's logical works had been studied in the
later days, and it happened that among the
last gifts of ancient Rome to literature were
commentaries on the *Categories* and *De Inter-
pretatione* by the great Boethius. How much
influence this one fact had on the course of
events may be disputed. What is certain is
that Western learning from the tenth century
onward can be seen laboriously building up a
knowledge of Aristotle, starting from these two
works and extending only slowly, first to the
other logical works, and then to the rest of his
writings. It is not till the middle of the twelfth
century that an instance can be found of the
completion of the first stage; and the further
extension beyond the *Organon* was wholly due,
before the recovery of a knowledge of Greek, to
the influence of the learned Arabs of Spain.
Through them it came about that the teaching
of Avicenna in Ispahan and Algazel in Bagdad
became known in the twelfth century to the
learned of the West.

By this devious path, from Athens to Constantinople, from Constantinople to Bagdad,
from Syria to Africa, from Africa to Spain,

came Aristotle to complete his empire in the West. And in what strange guise he came! The West knew no Greek and was far enough out in the interpretation of what it had received through the Latin. But Averroës was an Arab born in Spain, who knew neither the Greek in which the philosopher wrote, nor the Syriac into which he had been first translated, who wrote, further, his own commentaries in Arabic, which the nations of the West could not understand. The printed editions of the works of Averroës, observes Renan,[28] give us " a Latin version of a Hebrew version of a commentary written on an Arabic version of a Syriac version of a Greek text." Apart from these linguistic complications, Arab learning had only a very partial and abstract view of ancient Greece. It knew only philosophical and scientific authors and fell into the most elementary mistakes as soon as outside knowledge was required. Tragedy, for example, was to Averroës panegyric and comedy denunciation, and both were found in the Koran, while elegy meant erotic poetry. It is not surprising that the fruits of Arab industry are of no intrinsic value to the modern student.

The commentaries of Averroës were the

parting gift of Arab learning to the West. When he died in 1198, he had been banished from Spain, and the study of Greek philosophy had been forbidden in the Moorish dominions. His commentaries, however, which cover the whole of Aristotle's works with the exception of the *Historia Animalium* and the *Politics,* were for the next hundred years and more, one of the most important influences on Christian thought. Bringing new material for study, they widened the scope of philosophical enquiry. Aristotle was no longer the mere logician: psychology and metaphysics, biology, astronomy, and the science of nature, were found to be no less at his command. In the latter part of the twelfth century enterprising scholars, dissatisfied with the dull tradition of Paris, made their way to Toledo to enrich themselves from this great storehouse. The translation of the Arabic treatises was undertaken. But the old tradition did not give in without a struggle. At Paris in 1210 the private and public reading of Aristotle's works on natural philosophy, or of commentaries on them, was forbidden; and five years later the papal legate, while prescribing the study of the logical works, forbade the study of the

Physics and *Metaphysics*. But these prohibitions were gradually withdrawn. The Christian world could hardly say, with Averroës, that Aristotle was " the only man whom God had permitted to attain the highest summit of perfection "; but they could and did come to accept him as the supreme authority in every branch of secular learning. And with him at first they almost identified Averroës, the Moor of Spain. "About the middle of the fourteenth century," says Dr. Sandys, " the Inceptor in Arts at the university of Paris was compelled to swear that he would teach nothing inconsistent with ' Aristotle and his commentator Averroës.' " [29]

In the course of the thirteenth century the knowledge of Aristotle was also increased from a fresher and less contaminated source than Moorish learning. The capture of Constantinople by the hosts of the Crusaders and Venetians in 1204 opened direct communication with that ancient capital of Greek civilization, and from that date in one work after another direct translations from the Greek begin to supersede the translations from Arabic. Early in the next century the first steps were taken towards establishing the study of the

Greek language in the West. As early as 1273 William of Moerbeke in Flanders translated into Latin some of the Greek commentaries and several of Aristotle's works. But for many generations a knowledge of Greek sufficient to make possible the translation of a Greek text was a very rare accomplishment. The works of Aristotle prescribed for study in Western Universities were read in Latin versions. Even Thomas Aquinas seems to have had only a very rudimentary acquaintance with the Greek language. He had, however, the wisdom to get help from those who knew it, and refused to rely on versions from the Arabic. Dante (1265–1321), who refers to Aristotle more frequently than to any other Greek or Latin author, seems to have known no Greek at all.

Thomas Aquinas (1226–1274) was an Italian of noble birth who joined the Dominican Order and so had the good fortune to become the pupil of Albertus Magnus in the Dominican School at Cologne. Albertus was a man of exceptional learning and industry, a systematic student and expositor of Aristotle, and acquainted with Aristotle's thought in its whole range. While still largely dependent on Arab work, he was in many cases able to supplement and correct it from other sources. He has been criticized as a mere compiler: " but," says Dr. Sandys,[30] " he may perhaps be regarded with greater justice as a man of rich and varied endowments, who in astronomy and chemistry sought for truth in nature, and who deserves full credit as the restorer of the study of Aristotle." But though he prepared the way for the triumph of Aristotelianism over Platonism and Neo-Platonism as the predominant factor in Christian philosophy, the decisive influence was that of his gifted Italian pupil. Thomas Aquinas, the Angelical Doctor of the Schools, after some centuries of partial eclipse, is now generally admitted to the select company of great philosophers. As a commentator on Aristotle he was far in advance of his time, not only in understanding, but also in knowledge and (despite ignorance of Greek) in the essentials of scholarship. But though he wrote commentaries on all the most important of Aristotle's works, he was not primarily or essentially an expositor at all. These were studies subsidiary to his main work of constructing a philosophy for himself. The famous altar-piece by Traini at Pisa, painted in 1345, shows Aristotle holding open his *Ethics,* on the left, and Plato, holding open his *Timaeus,* on the right of the central figure of St. Thomas. Averroës lies vanquished and despairing beneath his feet. Another powerful influence, not there depicted, was that of Augustine. But in fact Aquinas did not swear allegiance to any one master. He attempted with success to effect a synthesis of the thought of the past as known to him.[31] Nevertheless, the popular view of him as an Aristotelian is amply justified, not merely by his services to the study of Aristotle, but also by the general cast and colour of his writings. If Aristotelianism ever lived outside Greece as a philosophic method, it lived in the Latin of the Angelical Doctor.

It was in Italy that the study of Greek first took root, and it was Italy that provided the last of the great schools of Aristotelian exegesis. For half a century before the fall of Constantinople in 1453 Greek scholars had been teaching their language to the enthusiastic youth of Italy. The surrender of the city to the Turkish invaders merely accelerated the process and swelled the tide of immigrants. For more than a hundred years Padua had already been a noted centre of Aristotelian learning. It had produced at the end of the thirteenth century one of the earliest translations from the Greek, and in the fourteenth Averroism found there its Italian home. Petrarch, who disliked Aristotle, disliked even more the Averroist Aristotelians of Padua, and is found urging on a friend to attack 'that mad dog Averroës.' Here the controversies between Thomists and Averroists continued bitterly for more than two hundred years after Aquinas' death, until at the end of the fifteenth century the Greek text was finally restored to its proper primacy and the great interpreters reduced to comparative insignificance. In this last period of its long life, when Averroism was almost forgotten, the school produced its masterpiece in the commentaries of Zabarella, who died in 1589. Writing at a time when a knowledge of Aristotle's logic and natural philosophy was universal among learned men, and when the advent of the printed book put the best authorities within easy reach, his commentaries may be said to represent the final climax of Aristotelianism in the Western world.

For, in general, Aristotle's reputation had been for some time declining. The Greeks brought other texts besides those of Aristotle, and in philosophy some, like those of Plato, far stronger in their immediate appeal to the new race of Greek scholars. At Paris in 1536 Ramus had maintained his celebrated thesis that all the doctrines of Aristotle were false. It was some compensation that the same year (as Dr. Sandys [99] remarks) saw the beginning of a rage for the *Poetics* in Italy. But modern science and modern philosophy were already germinating while Zabarella wrote; and as the real Aristotle at last came into view out of the mists of legend and tradition, the human spirit threw off his authority. The substance could not hold the empire which the shadow had won.

But the empire did not collapse without a struggle. It is true that the systematic study and exposition of the Aristotelian philosophy hardly outlived the sixteenth century, and that only a few continental seminaries wholeheartedly continued the old tradition. In the seventeenth century enquiry had new fields to explore. But the dogma of Aristotelian infallibility died hard, and many a modernist found himself in violent collision with it. In France, Peter Ramus was visited with the royal displeasure for his innovations in logic, and was prohibited by Francis I under pain of corporal punishment from " uttering any more slanderous invectives against Aristotle and other ancient authors received and approved." As late as 1624 it is recorded that the Parliament of Paris passed a decree in favour of the doctrines of Aristotle by way of rebuke to three philosophers who were accused of promulgating theses betraying a lack of respect for his sovereign authority. The decree followed the royal precedent, but was more severe in its terms, prohibiting all persons, under pain of death, " from holding or teaching any maxim contrary to the ancient and approved authors." " It thus appears," comments D'Alembert, recalling earlier prohibitions of Aristotelian heresies, " that there is really no sort of folly into which the philosophy of Aristotle has not led our good ancestors." [33] Thus it was not without trouble and difficulty that the seventeenth century threw off authority and laid the foundations of modern thought.[34]

In addition to such general proscriptions, there was no doubt much formal and informal persecution of individuals, during these centuries of transition, among the innovators great and small whose efforts laid the foundations of modern thought. Every history tells us that it was 'the Aristotelians' who drove Giordano Bruno from Paris in 1583 and Galileo from Pisa in 1591. But 'Aristotelian' in such connexions means little more than a claim to orthodoxy and a belief in the geocentric hypothesis. Such Aristotelianism has hardly more connexion with the great Schoolmen than with Aristotle himself. But it was the easier in those days for shocked and vindictive orthodoxy to take cover behind the name of Aristotle, because the scholarship of the time disowned it. The great scholars of the Renaissance tended to follow Petrarch's example both in the dislike and in the neglect of Aristotle. Erasmus, nearing the end of his life, wrote a preface to the Basle text of 1531, but does not appear otherwise to have written or thought much about him. The most Aristotelian of the great humanists was Erasmus' friend and contemporary, the Spaniard Juan Luis de Vivès, who taught for a time at Oxford, but mainly at Louvain, and edited the *De Anima*. But in general Aristotle was neglected. He stood no doubt, to these champions of *bonae literae*, for that stifling dialectical education from which the schools were crying for release.

The transition is well seen in England by a comparison of the attitude toward Aristotle of leading thinkers of successive periods, such as Bacon, Hobbes, Locke, and Berkeley. The Aristotle on whom Bacon lavishes his terse and eloquent, but not always well-informed invective, is the Aristotle of the Schoolmen, whose dogmatic solutions of the problems of nature, accepted as authoritative, bar the way to the free and fearless scrutiny of experience by which alone progress in these matters can come. Some of his accusations, no doubt, could be maintained against the real Aristotle, but most would have to be seriously modified and many altogether withdrawn. Hobbes, on the other hand, whose Oxford days fall in the early years of the seventeenth century, has both Aristotles very much in mind. He writes, in 1640,[35] of "him, whose opinions are at this day, and in these parts, of greater authority than any human writings"; and he takes pains to show that neither this nor any other authority runs with him. He criticizes Aristotle freely, for his ill opinion of monarchs, his subjection of the sovereign to law, his belief in the natural inequality of men, and on many another point of doctrine. He sneers at his

uncouth terminology and general obscurity —
so useful and convenient to scholastic theo-
logians — and treats his works often as the mere
" canting of Grecian sophisters." [36]   In the
Preface to the *Elements of Philosophy* (1655)[37]
he claims that astronomy and natural philosophy have only just begun, citing Copernicus,
Galileo, Harvey (" the only man I know, that,
conquering envy, hath established a new doctrine in his lifetime "), Kepler, Gassendi, and
Mersenne.   " Natural Philosophy is therefore
but young; but Civil Philosophy is yet much
younger, as being no older (I say it provoked,
and that my detractors may know how little
they have wrought upon me) than my own
book *De Cive*.   But what? were there no
philosophers natural or civil among the ancient
Greeks?   There were men so called; witness
Lucian, by whom they are derided; witness
divers cities, from which they have been often
by public edict banished.   But it follows not
that there was *philosophy*.   There walked in
old Greece a certain phantasm, for superficial
gravity, though full within of fraud and filth,
a little like philosophy; which unwary men,
thinking to be it, adhered to the professors
of it, some to one, some to another, though

[137]

they disagreed among themselves, and with great salary put their children to them to be taught, instead of wisdom, nothing but to dispute, and, neglecting the laws, to determine every question according to their own fancies." The monstrous union with the truths of Holy Scripture of this "babbling philosophy of Aristotle and other Greeks" has produced that 'metaphysical Empusa,' school divinity, not wholly confined to the Church of Rome, which Hobbes proposes to banish "not by skirmish, but by letting in the light upon her."

This, however, is only one side of the picture. With the Aristotle of the Schools, with the dogma of Aristotelian infallibility, there was to be no truce; the Aristotelian cosmos, again, had plainly fallen to pieces in the light of recent advances in science; and the lessons of Greek city life could only mislead seventeenth century Europe. Nevertheless, no philosophical writings had been more carefully studied by Hobbes than the works of Aristotle, and none had left a deeper mark upon his thinking. It may be doubted whether any English philosopher is as deeply and directly in his debt. Hobbes refers expressly and with respect to most of the more important treatises, and his

more psychological discussions are packed
with phrases borrowed without acknowledge-
ment from the *De Anima* and the *Parva Natu-
ralia*.[38]   A late work, the first of the ten dialogues on *Natural Philosophy*,[39] discussing the
origin and purpose of the enquiry, betrays
some consciousness of this debt.   Philosophy
has been treated as a trade, a fashion, an ele-
gant accomplishment, a mere means to prefer-
ment.   " And some, but few, there be, that
have studied it for curiosity and the delight
which commonly men have in the acquisition
of science and in the mastery of difficult and
subtil doctrines.   Of this last sort I count
Aristotle and a few others of the ancients, and
some few moderns: and to these it is that
properly belong the praises which are given to
philosophy."

Locke, if his own view of himself is to be
trusted, had much less appetite for book-learn-
ing and ancient subtleties than Hobbes.   He
never claimed more than a bowing acquaintance with any book, except perhaps the Bible,
and certainly made no profound study of the
works of Aristotle.   As a student at Oxford
during the Commonwealth he found, to his dis-
gust, that " the Aristotle of the Schoolmen,"

in Dr. Fraser's words,[40] " still determined the studies of the place." The paths of this philosophy seemed to him " perplexed with obscure terms and useless questions." Anthony Wood, a contemporary, reports that he was " ever prating and troublesome " and disdained to take notes at lectures. What Locke endured with such ill grace was no doubt the lees of the scholastic tradition. It is not to be supposed that the College tutors of his day had made a study of the philosopher's works. It was not Greek scholarship in any form, but the scientific work of Boyle, Sydenham, Huygens, and Newton, assisted perhaps by the novelty of the speculations of Descartes, which made Locke apologize for attempting " to instruct this our knowing age." [41] The tide of modern discovery had risen and was still rising; and it was the spirit of the time, rather than any personal idiosyncrasy, that led Locke to neglect the study of Aristotle and produced the tone of almost complete detachment from previous speculation which marks the pages of the *Essay on Human Understanding*. Fifty years later Hume showed himself a true follower of Locke when he described his *Treatise* as " an attempt to introduce the experimental method into the Moral Sciences." Why should the Moral Sciences study the past any more than the Physical Sciences did? Why should they not argue direct from experience like them?

Berkeley was born in Ireland in 1685, fifty-three years after Locke and ninety-seven after Hobbes. He studied at Trinity College, Dublin, where the classical tradition was always strong. At the time he wrote, a knowledge of Aristotle's writings was by no means common among philosophical writers in the British Isles. The works of course were available, printed in the original Greek and in translation; but during the eighteenth century few made any serious attempt to grapple with the central doctrines. Outlying portions of the corpus continued to be widely read. Statesmen as well as writers would occasionally take a hint from the *Politics*; and traces of an acquaintance with the *Ethics* and the *Rhetoric* are fairly common in the literature of the century. Further, the *Poetics*, which was practically unknown to the Middle Ages, was now the object of enthusiastic study, and influenced the literary practice of hundreds who had never set eyes on the tract itself. The result was that Berkeley was able to study and use Aristotle much as a writer of the present day might study and use him. The dogma of Aristotelian infallibility comes in for no more than a passing mention as a historical fact. Indeed, at the age of sixty, in his *Siris*, Berkeley is led, not for the first time, to plead with his age for a renewed study of Greek wisdom.[42] " Albeit in these days the depths of that old learning are rarely fathomed; and yet it were happy for these lands if our young nobility and gentry, instead of modern maxims, would imbibe the notions of the great men of antiquity. But, in these freethinking times, many an empty head is shook at Aristotle and Plato, as well as at the Holy Scriptures. And the writings of those celebrated ancients are by most men treated on a foot with the dry and barbarous lucubrations of the schoolmen." Such protests, however, were of no avail. The restoration of the study of Greek philosophy was a task reserved for the nineteenth century.

But the influence of Aristotle on modern thought is not to be measured solely by the extent to which his works have been studied, or by the continuing prestige of his name. In the course of centuries he had so embedded himself in the educational system of Europe that if none had read his works, he would still have long remained a power without parallel. "Those who have not followed him," complained Descartes,[43] " (amongst whom many of the best minds are to be found) have yet been imbued with his teaching in their youth, for it forms the sole teaching in the Schools." This was written in the middle of the seventeenth century, at the beginning of a period of rapid change, and by one who owed his education to the Roman Catholic priesthood. But even in Protestant England there was one subject at least in which Aristotelian influence was paramount, and was to remain paramount almost to the present day. This subject was Logic. Throughout the centuries logical compendia have continued to distil for the youth of schools and universities a predominantly Aristotelian tradition. The tradition has been sometimes more and sometimes less corrupt, but it has been without doubt, in spite of all corruptions, the strongest and most abiding, as well as the oldest and most pervasive, factor in the Aristotelian domination.

Aristotle was first known to the western

world as a logician. It is said of St. Ambrose, the fourth century Bishop of Milan, that he added to the Litany the petition — " From the Logic of Aristotle, deliver us, good Lord." [44] Whether the logical treatises were ever widely studied in the original Greek in the British Universities may be doubted; but certainly they were not in the seventeenth and eighteenth centuries, as well as for about half of the nineteenth. Yet the Universities, in which logic survived at all, did not enjoy the deliverance for which St. Ambrose prayed. An *Edinburgh Review* article of 1833 by Sir William Hamilton [45] throws some light on the position in the early nineteenth century. In Scotland, he complains, " the chairs of Logic have for generations taught anything rather than the science which they nominally profess," and Scotsmen have lost their reputation in a study in which they were once preëminent. In Cambridge logic is at an end, and " mathematics are there at length left to supply the discipline which logic was of old supposed exclusively to afford." Oxford is described as " the only British seminary where the study of logic proper can be said to have survived "; and the article is devoted to a review of a number of logical works emanating from that university. Sir William Hamilton convicts the writers, one and all, of ignorance: " not one," he says, " seems to have studied the logical treatises of Aristotle," to say nothing of the Greek commentators or of the continental logicians of more recent times. By statute, he observes, the Oxford professor of Dialectic was obliged to expound the *Organon* twice weekly: but the statutory system had been superseded: the professors (as Gibbon had discovered in 1752) had altogether ceased to perform their duties. Logic was taught in Oxford by the College Tutors from Latin compendia, eclectic compilations by authors ignorant of the source of the doctrines they expounded, devoid of any impulse to original speculation, and contaminating tradition only by an occasional more or less happy exercise of mother wit. " The Compendium of Sanderson (1615) stood its ground for a season, when the more elaborate treatises (erst in academical use) of Brerewood, Crackanthorpe, and Smiglecius, were forgotten. But this little treatise, the excellent work of an accomplished logician, was too closely relative to the books of the *Organon*, and demanded too frequently an inconvenient explanation, to retain its place, so soon as another text-book could be introduced, more accomodated to the fallen and falling standard of tutorial competency. Such a text-book was soon found in the Compendium of Aldrich. . . . The book — which, in justice to the Dean, we ought to mention was not originally written for the public — is undoubtedly a work of no inconsiderable talent; but the talent is, perhaps, principally shown in the author having performed so cleverly a task for which he was so indifferently prepared. Absolutely considered, it has little or no value." It is interesting to note that the last edition of Dean Aldrich's work, first published in 1691, appeared in 1862, but enriched with a learned commentary by Mansel of St. John's (later Dean of St. Paul's), who earned the commendation of Sir William Hamilton, and did more than anyone of his time for the establishment of the study of Greek and German philosophy in his university.

The study of Aristotle was in fact reviving as Sir William Hamilton wrote. The publication of the Berlin edition of Aristotle's works was almost contemporaneous with that of the article. Study of Aristotle soon revealed the fact that the more solid and durable elements in the logical tradition were derived from Aristotle himself; and on one side at least, 'back to Aristotle' has been the most fruitful formula in the recent reconstruction of logical studies. Other influences were of course at work during the nineteenth century to revivify the subject; and modern text-books do not succeed in completely harmonizing new and old. But at any rate logic is now once more recognized as an essential part of philosophy; and to that result the renewed study of the Aristotelian sources have largely contributed. These same enquiries have also been effective to straighten the path of the student of elementary logic, so common in the modern universities. Misunderstandings have been removed, unnecessary accretions swept away; and even a student ignorant of Greek can, if he wishes, without great difficulty reach an understanding of the main positions.

The sifting and winnowing which academic writers have exercised upon the text-books of Logic, restoring in the process the original Aristotelian framework, had in a sense already been carried out by educated men in the daily use of writing and conversation. The efforts of nineteenth century scholars are too recent to have left as yet any considerable mark upon the terms of ordinary speech and thought. But these terms show little trace of scholastic refinements or later academic pedantries. They include, however, the Latin equivalent of nearly every central term in the Aristotelian vocabulary. Quantity and quality, form and matter, substance and essence have international currency in the fabric of ordinary speech. Few may have heard of the ' Predicables,' but most attach a more or less exact meaning to definition, genus, species, differentia, property, accident. Critics untrained in logic speak freely of axioms and postulates, of principles and premises and conclusions, demand a more rigorous ' demonstration,' or protest that an argument ' begs the question.' Indeed, in the terms of popular logic Aristotle has almost a monopoly (another Aristotelian word); and in no direction can a modern European think to any purpose without the assistance of terms which Aristotle either brought into currency or re-minted to his own liking.

To this result the direct influence of the more popular writings, the *Ethics, Politics, Poetics, Rhetoric,* has no doubt contributed. But their influence has been as nothing compared with

that of a logic, — based ultimately on that of
Aristotle, but taught mostly under other names
by persons who admitted no allegiance to the
Greek philosopher, — which ensured that men
should speak the language which he had invented, even when they repudiated the doctrines which they supposed him to have maintained.

There is no way of estimating the far-reach-
ing effects of this unbroken tradition, without
parallel in the history of thought. A philosophical idea can be tracked to its source and
followed in its successive developments, but
a term is infinitely subtle in its suggestions,
and escapes for the most part our rough
measures. It is only, as a rule, when we
speak a foreign language that we notice ourselves saying, not so much what we intended,
as what we have words for. Yet the *patrii
sermonis egestas* is an ever present fact, a
force not banished by remaining normally un-
noticed. It would be fruitless to consider what
modern thought might have been, if Aristotle
had not written or had not been read. It is
sufficient to note that the Aristotelian contribution is, not so much any doctrine or body
of doctrine, as a contribution to the stuff of

thought itself. And indeed, what more could be said? Could there be a more conclusive proof of the efficacy of a philosophy than the ubiquity of its phraseology, more than two thousand years later, in the mouths of men — of men who may never have studied it, who are not trying to state or echo it, but are think- ing their own thoughts and unravelling in their own way the general and special problems of life and nature? Of the doctrine of Aristotle little has ever reached the market-place. Many have heard that he thought virtue a mean; and the better-informed are aware of a rather ob- scure phrase connecting tragedy with the emo- tions of pity and fear. The name carries no suggestion of sublime mysticism, like that of his master Plato, or of ambitious speculative construction, like that of Hegel and many another modern philosopher. It is as imper- sonal and inevitable as that of Shakespeare. Which is a fair measure of our Aristotelianism.

Strabo says of Posidonius that his more physical speculations are not worthy of great attention: " for there is so much causal ex- planation and Aristotelianism in him, which we decline to attempt because of the obscurity

of the causes." [46]   Strabo wrote in the first
century of our era, and speaks for the Stoics of
his time.   When he writes of causes, he has
in mind, of course, not the Epicurean ancestor
of Mill's 'invariable antecedent,' but Aristotle's four causes or reasons, and especially
the Form and the End.   A modern scientist,
confronted with Aristotle's scientific works,
would say much the same, though he would
phrase it differently.   When Francis Bacon [47]
complains that Aristotle enslaved natural philosophy to logic and made experience the tor-
tured captive of his own prepossessions, he is
expressing a similar suspicion based on a
rather slight acquaintance with the works criticized.   And when Hobbes [48] still in the time
of Cromwell finds it necessary to indulge in
similar diatribes, it is the belief in 'Entities
and Essences' or 'Substantial Forms' that
he chooses for the main point of attack.   It
is this, with the assumption of Aristotelian infallibility, that makes the study which "is
not properly philosophy, but Aristotelity."   In
these writers, even as late as Hobbes, there is
still some confusion between the real Aristotle
and the Aristotle of the schoolmen: but, so
far as there is a real point at issue between

Aristotle and the precursors of modern science, it is not ill put by Bacon when he opposes the intellect let loose in speculation to the patient accumulation of the evidence of fact by which alone in his opinion truth is capable of being attained.

Yet this opposition does not carry us far. Rashness in hypothesis is not the prerogative of any age or time: it is rather the sign of a hopeful spirit, and perhaps constitutes a useful or even necessary phase in the early development of any science. In his own day certainly Aristotle was not more open than others to such a charge. He was peculiar rather for the immense industry with which he collected and studied all available evidence on the matters with which he dealt. The Time-Spirit had no doubt brought to birth in Bacon's generation an idea lacking not only in Aristotle but in the whole ancient world — the idea of a great realm of knowledge open to conquest by the coöperative effort of ordinary men trained in the method of observation and experiment. On some such basis modern science rests. But we do not yet know how far this alone will take us. 'Entities and Essences' and 'Substantial Forms' may have little attraction for modern science, but it may nevertheless be doubted whether they have been finally banished from the thought of men. It is not inapposite, perhaps, to recall the words with which Lotze closed his *Logic* in 1874, when the reaction against the Hegelian idealism was at its height. He admits that Hegel's ' audacious flight' was hampered by the incompleteness of its empirical foundation. He admits that it erred in representing as attained or attainable what can only be the final goal of completed knowledge. " But," he adds, " in view of the universal idolatry of experience which prevails at present, and which is all the cheaper and all the safer now that the importance and indispensableness of its object are visible to all mankind, I will at least close with the avowal that I hold the much reviled ideal of speculative intuition to be the supreme and not wholly unattainable goal of science, and with the expression of my hope that German philosophy will always rouse itself afresh, with more of moderation and reserve, yet with no less enthusiasm, to the endeavour, not merely to *calculate* the course of the world, but to *understand* it." This defence of Hegel is also the defence of

Aristotle and of every other great speculative thinker.

The quotation suggests a final question. 'Hegelian' and 'Hegelianism' are terms in common use, as indicative of a certain speculative tendency. 'Aristotelian' and 'Aristotelianism' not only are not so used to-day, but appear never to have been so used in the history of philosophy. Platonism is to Plato much what Hegelianism is to Hegel; but there has been no analogous Aristotelianism. The tendency ascribed by Strabo to Posidonius is merely a similarity of method in dealing with physical problems. Hobbes' 'Aristotelity' is a study of Aristotle's writings with submission to his authority. Perhaps in view of 'the obscurity of the causes' we ought, with the Stoics, to decline to explore the reason for the difference. But a suggestion will do no harm. Aristotle was an encyclopaedic writer, and for that reason alone not easily summed up in a formula. He was more interested in the conspectus of knowledge than in controversy with rival philosophers. He scarcely ever presents his own view as the affirmation of something which others deny, or as the denial of something others affirm. He distinguishes, he mediates oppositions, guided through all by a profound belief in the sanity of the human intelligence and by the desire to preserve in his own statement as much as possible of what his predecessors have said. No man was ever less of a partisan. If any man ever had the central mind, he had it. Such a mind does not found a school; but it is well fitted for other services. It was well fitted to guide the modern world through its infancy, to give it a scientific vocabulary, and, when its authority was nominally abrogated, still by means of this vocabulary and its rich associations, as well as in more direct ways, to act as a moderating and centralizing influence on the controversies of later generations. Aristotle, in short, could be no man's master because he was to be the master of all. " No one," says Schelling,[49] " will create anything enduring who has not come to terms with Aristotle, and sharpened his own ideas on the whetstone of his arguments." But perhaps in saying this Schelling goes too far. No man or book is indispensable; and it is Aristotle's special glory that every thinker is his pupil, even when he does not know it.

NOTES AND BIBLIOGRAPHY

NOTES

1. Cf. Pauly-Wissowa, *Real-Encyclopaedie*, Art., "Aristoteles" (Gercke).

2. For various reasons an Aristotelian treatise presents a very different kind of unity from a modern book, and terminology suitable to the latter can be used only with certain reservations. The generalization may be hazarded that in modern times, ideally at least, a treatise is required to exhibit, besides objective unity (*i.e.* that derived from the matter treated of), a certain subjective or artistic unity: like any work of art, it should have — in Aristotle's own phrase — a beginning, a middle, and an end; while in ancient times a scientific work was released from the latter requirement. The question, however, is too complicated to be disposed of in a short note. The Aristotelian problem is handled in masterly fashion in Jaeger's *Entstehungsgeschichte der Metaphysik des Aristoteles.*

3. *Life and Letters*, III, p. 252.

4. It is of course not credible that Aristotle should have composed all the corpus during his short time at the Lyceum. Even on the surface it is in fact evident that manuscripts of different dates were put together to compose many of the treatises. But little attempt has been made till lately to discriminate the various strata and reconstruct the history of Aristotle's development as a whole. An entirely new face has been put upon this question by the bold and suggestive treatment of it in Prof. Jaeger's recent *Aristoteles* (1923). It is probable that certain portions of the surviving works date back to the period of Aristotle's membership of the Academy, when he was a professed Platonist. Larger portions were composed or reduced to their present form during Aristotle's stay in Asia Minor. There, if Jaeger is right, he

conducted his first school, in a spirit of critical loyalty to the Academy, and attempted to formulate a reformed Platonism. On these foundations during the last period he built up his mature thought, and confirmed his principles by exhibiting them in a variety of new applications. A simple formula, such as that his development was from mysticism to positivism, or from transcendence to immanence, or from metaphysics to matter of fact, is more easily invented than justified. The whole material needs to be worked over afresh in the light of the new ideas. For a timely and illuminating survey of the position see Prof. J. Burnet's lecture, " Aristotle," in the *Proceedings of the British Academy* for 1924 (Vol. XI).

5. *Geogr.*, p. 618. ' Learned ' is not quite a fair translation of the Greek word (λογίους), which suggests rather fertility in exposition and explanation. But books had not yet piled themselves into mountains, and the erudite bookworm (our modern glory) could not exist.

6. *Phaedo*, 96–100, somewhat abridged.

7. *Metaph.*, Bk. I. Translation and Commentary by A. E. Taylor, *Aristotle on his Predecessors,* Chicago, Open Court, 1907.

8. Prof. J. Burnet and Prof. A. E. Taylor, both of St. Andrews, are the chief representatives of this ' heresy.' Burnet's *Greek Philosophy, Part I: Thales to Plato,* London, 1914, gives the best general statement of the position.

9. Plato, *Parmenides,* 130.

10. *Cratylus,* 389; *Republic,* 597.

11. *Metaph.*, M4, 1078b9.

12. A general account of Aristotle's theory of form and matter is bound to draw upon many of his works. The most fundamental passages in this connexion are to be found in the *Posterior Analytics* and in the central books of the *Metaphysics*. A masterly exposition of the resulting conception of the science of nature is given in the Introduction to Prof. H. H. Joachim's edition of the *De Gen. et Corr., Aristotle on Coming-to-be and Passing-away,* Oxford, 1922.

13. Plato, *Timaeus,* 52B.

14. The most striking instance is that of the female sex, which, however necessary to the existence of the species, must nevertheless be regarded as a deviation from nature in the sense explained.

15. *Metaph.*, Λ7, 1072b13.

16. The material of this chapter is mainly drawn from the *De Caelo,* which is not, as its name suggests, an account merely of the heavenly bodies, but rather of all ' simple bodies.'

17. *De Caelo,* I 270b14. Simplicius, commenting on this passage, says that he ' has been told ' that there are written astronomical records in Egypt for the past 630,000 years and in Babylon for the past 1,440,000 years!

18. No estimate of the number of spheres required is given in the *De Caelo:* the text is based on *Metaph.* Λ8, 1073b17. A detailed account of Eudoxus' theory and of Aristotle's relation to it will be found in Sir Thomas Heath's *Aristarchus of Samos,* pp. 190–248. Eudoxus of Cnidus was intermediate in age between Plato and Aristotle. In the histories of philosophy he is not reckoned as a Platonist, but as a Pythagorean. As a mathematician, if Heath is right, he had no equal in antiquity except Archimedes.

19. *De Caelo,* II. 12, 292a14–b26, slightly abridged (Oxford translation).

20. The sources for this section are of course the various treatises on animals.

21. This chapter is based mainly on the *De Anima* and the *Nicomachean Ethics.*

22. Cf. Shakespeare, *Troilus and Cressida,* II. ii. 163–67:
" Paris and Troilus, you have both said well;
And on the cause and question now in hand
Have glozed, but superficially; not much
Unlike young men, whom Aristotle thought
Unfit to hear moral philosophy."

23. Epicharmus, fr. 20 (Diels, *Vorsokratiker,* 13B).

24. The material of this chapter is drawn from the *Politics.*

25. This chapter is mainly based on Sir J. E. Sandys'

fascinating *History of Classical Scholarship,* to which the reader is referred for further information on many of the points raised.

26. Strabo, *Geogr.,* p. 608 f.; Plutarch, *Sulla,* 26; Athenaeus, 3a and 214a.

27. For this and the following paragraph, cf. Jaeger, *Entstehungsgeschichte,* p. 176.

28. *Averroës et l'Averroïsme,* Ed. 2, p. 52.

29. *Hist. of Classical Scholarship,* I,³ p. 604 (with the reservation, however, given in Sandys' footnote — ' save in defence of the Faith ').

30. *Ib.,* p. 581.

31. For an exceedingly interesting account of the relation of Thomism to the thought of Plato and Aristotle, see *Saint Thomas Aquinas as a Philosopher,* by A. E. Taylor, Oxford, Blackwell, 1924 (Aquinas Sexcentenary Lecture).

32. *Ib.,* II, p. 133.

33. Thomas Brown, *Lectures on the Philosophy of the Human Mind, Edinburgh,* 1828, p. 284.

34. An article by Prof. R. S. Rait in the *English Historical Review,* XIV. 250–260 (1899), entitled " Andrew Melville and the Revolt against Aristotle in Scotland," gives a good idea of the troubles attending the introduction of the new learning, during the last quarter of the sixteenth century, into the Scottish Universities. When Melville began his work, ' Aristotle ' was in full possession; but it is noted that the champions of Aristotle had read few of his works, and those not in the Greek. Melville had studied under Ramus, and was much given to proving, like him, that Aristotle could err. He disliked metaphysics; and his reforms seem to have tended, for the time at least, to the discouragement of philosophical study generally.

35. *English Works* (Molesworth), IV. 102.

36. *Ib.,* IV. 181.

37. *Ib.,* I. viii. ff.

38. See list of parallels given by J. Freudenthal, *Ueber den Begriff des Wortes φαντασία bei Aristoteles,* Goettingen, 1863, p. 24n.

39. *English Works*, VII. 72.

40. In his edition of the *Essay*, I, p. xix.

41. In the 'Epistle to the Reader,' prefixed to the *Essay*.

42. *Siris*, par. 332.

43. *The Philosophical Works of Descartes*, 2 vols., trans. by E. S. Haldane and G. R. T. Ross, Cambridge, England, 1911–12; Vol. I, p. 207.

44. Quoted by Sir William Hamilton on the authority of Nicholas of Cusa.

45. Reprinted in Hamilton's *Discussions on Philosophy*, New York, 1853.

46. *Geogr.*, p. 104.

47. *Novum Organum*, I. 63, and many other passages.

48. *Leviathan*, chapter xlvi.

49. *Werke*, XI. 380.

BIBLIOGRAPHY

1. Works.

A complete translation of these is in course of preparation at the Oxford University Press, edited by W. D. Ross. Many of the most important of the works are already published, including *Metaphysics, De Caelo, De Generatione et Corruptione, Politics,* and the great zoölogical treatises.

2. General.

ADAMSON, ROBERT, *The Development of Greek Philosophy.* Edinburgh and London, 1908.

JAEGER, W. W., *Aristoteles: Grundlegung einer Geschichte seiner Entwicklung.* Berlin, 1923.

Ross, W. D., *Aristotle.* New York, 1924.

SIEBECK, HERMANN, *Aristoteles* [4]. Stuttgart, 1922. Cf. c. 8. " Fortleben."

TAYLOR, A. E., *Aristotle* [2], in Series, " The People's Books." London and New York, 1919.

ZELLER, E., *Aristotle and The Earlier Peripatetics.* Translation by B. F. C. Costelloe and J. H. Muirhead. 2 vols. London and New York, 1897.

3. Special.

Logic and Metaphysics.

ADAMSON, ROBERT, *Short History of Logic.* Edinburgh, 1911.

JOHNSON, EDITH H., *Argument of Aristotle's Metaphysics.* New York, 1906.

MAIER, HEINRICH, *Die Syllogistik des Aristoteles.* 3 vols. Tuebingen, 1900.

Science of Nature.

BAEUMKER, CLEMENS, *Das Problem der Materie in der Griechischen Philosophie.* Münster, 1890.

BIBLIOGRAPHY

HEATH, SIR THOMAS, *Aristarchus of Samos, the Ancient Copernicus.* Oxford, 1913.

Psychology.

BEARE, JOHN I., *Greek Theories of Elementary Cognition, From Alcmaeon to Aristotle.* Oxford, 1906.

Politics and Ethics.

BARKER, SIR ERNEST, *The Political Thought of Plato and Aristotle.* London and New York, 1906.

BURNET, JOHN, *Aristotle on Education.* Cambridge, 1905.

NEWMAN, W I., *The Politics of Aristotle.* (Introduction, Text, Essays, Notes.) 4 vols. Oxford, 1887–1902.

VINOGRADOFF, SIR PAUL, *Outlines of Historical Jurisprudence.* 2 vols. Oxford, 1920–22.

4. Composition and History.

CHRIST, WILHELM VON, *Geschichte der Griechischen Litteratur,* in I. von Müller: *Handbuch der Klassischen Altertumswissenschaft,* VII. 1. Ed. 6., § 368. "Fortleben des Aristoteles." Munich, 1912.

JAEGER, W. W., *Studien zur Entstehungsgeschichte der Metaphysik des Aristoteles.* Berlin, 1912.

SANDYS, SIR J. E., *A History of Classical Scholarship.* 3 vols. Cambridge, England, 1903–8.

SHUTE, RICHARD, *On the history of the process by which the Aristotelian writings arrived at their present form.* Oxford, 1888.

WENDELL, BARRETT, *Traditions of European Literature, From Homer to Dante.* New York, 1920.

AUTHORS AND TITLES

HOMER. *John A. Scott.*

SAPPHO. *David M. Robinson.*

EURIPIDES. *F. L. Lucas.*

ARISTOPHANES. *Louis E. Lord.*

DEMOSTHENES. *Charles D. Adams.*

THE POETICS OF ARISTOTLE. *Lane Cooper.*

GREEK RHETORIC AND LITERARY CRITICISM. *W. Rhys Roberts.*

LUCIAN. *Francis G. Allinson.*

CICERO AND HIS INFLUENCE. *John C. Rolfe.*

CATULLUS. *Karl P. Harrington.*

LUCRETIUS AND HIS INFLUENCE. *George Depue Hadzsits.*

OVID. *Edward Kennard Rand.*

HORACE. *Grant Showerman.*

VIRGIL. *John William Mackail.*

SENECA THE PHILOSOPHER. *Richard Mott Gummere.*

APULEIUS. *Elizabeth Hazelton Haight.*

MARTIAL. *Paul Nixon.*

PLATONISM. *Alfred Edward Taylor.*

ARISTOTELIANISM. *John L. Stocks.*

STOICISM. *Robert Mark Wenley.*

LANGUAGE AND PHILOLOGY. *Roland G. Kent.*

AUTHORS AND TITLES

AESCHYLUS AND SOPHOCLES. *J. T. Sheppard.*

GREEK RELIGION. *Walter Woodburn Hyde.*

SURVIVALS OF ROMAN RELIGION. *Gordon J. Laing.*

MYTHOLOGY. *Jane Ellen Harrison.*

ANCIENT BELIEFS IN THE IMMORTALITY OF THE SOUL. *Clifford H. Moore.*

STAGE ANTIQUITIES. *James Turney Allen.*

PLAUTUS AND TERENCE. *Gilbert Norwood.*

ROMAN POLITICS. *Frank Frost Abbott.*

PSYCHOLOGY, ANCIENT AND MODERN. *G. S. Brett.*

ANCIENT AND MODERN ROME. *Rodolfo Lanciani.*

WARFARE BY LAND AND SEA. *Eugene S. McCartney.*

THE GREEK FATHERS. *James Marshall Campbell.*

GREEK BIOLOGY AND MEDICINE. *Henry Osborn Taylor.*

MATHEMATICS. *David Eugene Smith.*

LOVE OF NATURE AMONG THE GREEKS AND ROMANS. *H. R. Fairclough.*

ANCIENT WRITING AND ITS INFLUENCE. *B. L. Ullman.*

GREEK ART. *Arthur Fairbanks.*

ARCHITECTURE. *Alfred M. Brooks.*

ENGINEERING. *Alexander P. Gest.*

MODERN TRAITS IN OLD GREEK LIFE. *Charles Burton Gulick.*

ROMAN PRIVATE LIFE. *Walton Brooks McDaniel.*

GREEK AND ROMAN FOLKLORE. *William Reginald Halliday.*

ANCIENT EDUCATION. *J. F. Dobson.*